Listen To This

Michael Frayn

LISTEN TO THIS
21 short plays and sketches

METHUEN

This collection first published in paperback in Great Britain in 1990 by Methuen London, Michelin House, 81 Fulham Road, London SW3 6RB and distributed in the United States of America by HEB Inc, 361 Hanover Street, Portsmouth, New Hampshire 03801.

A CIP catalogue record for this book is available from The British Library.

ISBN 0 413 64420 0

The front and back cover images are by Brian Grimwood
The photograph of Michael Frayn on the back cover is © Jillian Edelstein

Listen to This, Confession, Blots, Value for Money, Who Do You Think You Are?, Glycerine, Heaven and *The Messenger's Assistant* were first seen in Eleanor Bron's television series *Beyond A Joke*, in 1972.

A Little Peace and Quiet and *Never Mind the Weather* have not been performed or published.

Black and Silver, The New Quixote, Mr Foot and *Chinamen* were originally performed together under the title *The Two of Us*. The production – by Michael Codron – was directed by Mark Cullingham and designed by Ken Calder. All the parts were performed by Richard Briers and Lynn Redgrave. It opened at the Garrick Theatre on 30 July 1970. The plays were originally published under the title *The Two of Us* by Fontana Books in 1970.

Head to Head first appeared in the *Guardian*, and is reproduced here by permission of the Editor. It was first published in book form in *The Book of Fub* (Collins, 1963). *A Pleasure Shared* first appeared in the *Independent*. The remaining four pieces first appeared in the *Observer*, and appear here by permission of the Editor. They were first published in book form in *On the Outskirts* (Collins, 1964).

An Occasion of this Nature was first performed by Eleanor Bron at an Amnesty evening (The Secret Policeman's Ball) in 1979.

Printed in England by Clays Ltd, St Ives plc

Contents

Listen to this

Husband Good God. Good God. (*Looks over the top of his newspaper at his* **Wife**.) Good God.
Wife (*lowers her newspaper*) Sorry?
Husband A woman at a funeral in Essex yesterday was knocked down and killed by the hearse.
Wife (*vaguely*) Good God.

They both return to their papers.

Husband (*without looking up*) The Chancellor's been sounding off about various things.
Wife (*without looking up*) Good God.
Husband Fares are going up again.
Wife Good God.
Husband (*surprised*) Good God

He lowers his paper and waits until she has lowered hers.

Wife What?
Husband You remember that man we met at the Wrights' last week? The tall chap with glasses? Something to do with educational publishing?
Wife Yes?
Husband Remember where his wife came from?
Wife No?
Husband Prestonpans. Just outside Edinburgh. I remember thinking at the time what an odd name it was. Well, they had a freak storm there yesterday.

She waits. He goes back to his paper.

Wife Is she all right?
Husband Is who all right?
Wife The wife of the man we met at the Wrights'?
Husband She doesn't live there *now*. Obviously. Since she lives *here*. But a number of trees were uprooted.

They read for a while.

	Good God! Do you know how much money people in this country spent on potato crisps last year?
Wife	(*without looking up*) Six million pounds.
Husband	Six million pounds!

He shakes his head and laughs, then looks up.

	What did you say?
Wife	I didn't say anything.
Husband	I thought you said something. You're always trying to tell me things when I'm reading.

They read. He laughs.

	How about this? 'An Electricity Board official said last night that the Board's computer had apparently gone hoywire.'
Wife	(*vaguely*) Good God.
Husband	(*stops laughing*) Oh. I'm talking to myself, am I?
Wife	No, I was listening. An official said the computer had gone haywire.
Husband	Hoywire.
Wife	That's obviously a misprint.
Husband	Yes.

He returns heavily to his paper. She looks at him.

Wife	Listen to this, then. 'Officials in La Paz were last night expressing cautious optimism about Paraguay's apparently more flexible line on talks. They were commenting on reports that Paraguay had dropped its insistence on the exclusion of relations with Chile from the agenda as a precondition for any meeting.'
Husband	What's funny about that?
Wife	Nothing at all.
Husband	Not very surprising, is it?
Wife	Not at all surprising.
Husband	We don't know anyone who lives in La Paz, do we?
Wife	I don't think so. There aren't any misprints, either.

I thought it would make a change from the news in your paper.

Husband (*goes back to reading his paper, hurt*) And I thought marriage was supposed to be something to do with sharing.

Confession

Penitent   What else? Well, I've been guilty of the sin of anger. I've shouted at my children several times during the past week. As Thou hast, of course, seen, with Thy All-Seeing Eye. And no doubt heard, with Thy All-Hearing Ear.

And then again I've committed malice on a number of occasions. I was definitely trying to hurt my sister's feelings that time. I mean on Tuesday. When my sister – this is my younger sister I'm talking about, Janice, the one who lives just outside Watford . . . Well, of course, Thou knowest which sister I mean. I always forget that with Thy All-Knowing Mind Thou knowest perfectly well what I mean. Much better than *I* do, in fact. I only went to see her on Tuesday at all, I have to confess, because I was over in that direction anyway, visiting Mother in the nursing home, which as Thou knowest I always try to do at least once a week – I mean, not of course that I want to boast about it – it's the very least I can do – in fact I feel terrible about not having her at home, as Thou knowest . . .

Or did I drop it into the conversation like that to make Thee think better of me? Well, Thou knowest whether I did or not, and if Thou thinkest I *did* then I repent it *at once*, as I try to do with *all* my unworthy thoughts and actions . . .

Hold on – where was I, before I got sidetracked like that? (Another of my faults, incidentally, for which I'm extremely sorry.) I was in the middle of repenting something . . . Well, Thou knowest perfectly well what I was going to say, so if I can't remember perhaps Thou couldst take it as repented all the same . . .

Oh no, I know, my sister. Yes, when she started to go on about Mother and Mrs Wemyss (who, as Thou knowest, runs the nursing home) and I said, 'Janice, I honestly do not want to sit here and listen to you going on about that woman, who has been so *kind* to Mother,' and Janice turned to me and gave me one of those looks of hers . . .

Well, of course, Thou sawest the whole incident. If I mention the words 'gooseberry jam' I'm sure Thou knowest exactly what I'm repenting of. And of course when I said how clever I thought her children's drawings were, Thou weren'test fooled for a moment. Nor was she, of course.

Anyway, I'm truly sorry. In fact I've been brooding about it ever since. And that's another thing I ought to mention – the way I think about myself all the time. I mean, whenever I'm not actually busy doing something wrong I'm thinking about how wrong it was. Dost Thou know what I mean? Well, of course Thou dost.

This seems to me to be my worst sin of all. I don't know whether Thou wouldst agree. Or wait a minute, though. Am I just thinking this as an excuse for *not* thinking perpetually about my sins? Anyway, *Thou* knowest for certain what I'm up to, and whatever it is I'm really and truly sorry about it. Aren't I?

At the Sign of the Rupture Belt

Nicolette   There's the shop with the rupture belt outside! Now we've driven halfway to Granny's, haven't we, Daddy?

Father   Halfway exactly.

Nicolette   I always remember we're halfway when we get to the shop with the rupture belt outside, don't I, Daddy?

Dominic   And I always remember we're three-quarters way when we get to Acme Motors, don't I, Daddy?

Mother   I wish you two would stop your silly pestering. I don't know why we bring you out in the car to Granny's.

Father   It's good for them to travel, Eileen. They see new things. They get something fresh to talk about.

Dominic   There's the factory with the rusty bike on the roof!

Nicolette   There's the advertisement for Viriloids Rejuvenating Pills!

Dominic   There's the Tigers!

Mother   The *what*?

Dominic   The Tigers! That's what we always call the Lyons there, don't we, Daddy?

Father   We certainly do, son. And there's the brewery where they brew the Adam's ale.

Nicolette   Daddy always says that now when we pass the Wemblemore waterworks, doesn't he, Dominic? He never used to, did he?

Father   What's this place on the right, children?

Dominic   I know! I know! It's the site for the new eye hospital.

Nicolette   Say your joke, Daddy, say your joke!

Father   It's a proper site for sore eyes.

Nicolette   Did you hear Daddy say his joke, Mummy?

Mother   Are we in Sudstow yet, John?

Dominic   Mummy, you *never* know where this is. You always ask Daddy if we're in Sudstow when we get to the site for sore eyes.

Father   Where are we then, Mr Knowall?

Dominic   We're just coming to the place where we saw the drunk men fighting –

Nicolette	– where Daddy always says: 'Can you imagine a more godforsaken hole than this?'
Dominic	And Mummy says she can't.
Father	We're just coming into Surley, Eileen.
Dominic	And you're not sure, are you, Daddy, but you think Wemblemore ends and Surley begins just after Wile-U-Wate Footwear Repairs, don't you?
Father	Look at it, Eileen. Scruffy people, cheapjack stores, rundown cinemas. I wonder how many pubs there are in this street alone?
Dominic	There are nine, Daddy.
Nicolette	We always count them for you.
Father	Can you imagine a more godforsaken hole?
Nicolette	Daddy said it, Dominic.
Dominic	Now say you can't, Mummy.
Mother	Oh, do stop pestering. Can't you think of some game to play as we go along?
Dominic	We *are* playing a game, Mummy. But you're not playing it properly.
Nicolette	You haven't said you can't imagine such a godforsaken hole, has she, Dominic?
Mother	Those children! They're enough to try the patience of a saint!
Father	There's Acme Motors, anyway – we're three-quarters of the way there now.
Dominic	*Daddy!* That's what *I* say! *I'm* the one who sees Acme Motors and says we're three-quarters of the way there!
Nicolette	Yes, Daddy, that's *Dominic's* thing to say!
Father	Well, I've said it now.
Nicolette	But that's not fair, Daddy! You say: 'I hope to God there's not going to be a holdup in Sudstow High Street'.
Dominic	You've *spoilt* it, Daddy, you've *spoilt* it! You've said my thing!
Nicolette	Now you've made Dominic cry.
Father	Calm down, Dominic. Be your age.
Dominic	How would you like it if I said your things? How would you like it if I said 'A site for sore eyes'?
Mother	Don't be disrespectful to your father, Dominic.
Dominic	I don't care! *A site for sore eyes! A site for sore eyes! A site for sore eyes!*

Mother	If you don't stop this instant, Dominic, I'm going to . . .
Nicolette	Daddy, Daddy! We've gone past Cook and Cook (Wholesale Tobacconists) and you haven't said your joke about spoiling the breath!
Father	Oh, dry up.
Mother	Now they're both howling. It's all your fault, John. They just copy you.
Father	That's what you always say.
Mother	And that's what *you* always say!
Father	Well, all I can say is, I hope to God there's not going to be a holdup in Sudstow High Street.

A Little Peace and Quiet

A garden. Sunshine. Two chairs.

Wife   He won't think of anything out here. I could tell him that. The lawn-sprinkler going all the time. The birds singing. It's not the right atmosphere. Not for him. Why doesn't he go inside? Get a bit of peace and quiet. It's ridiculous. Every day. Sitting here. Sitting in the kitchen watching me give Mrs Henty her instructions. No wonder he can't think of anything.

Husband   He's talking to them again. Talking to the dogs. I've never heard of that, talking to guard-dogs. They should be like wild animals. They shouldn't be talked to. What does he say to them?

Wife   That play about the blind beggar. He didn't think of that sitting in a garden listening to the birds. It was in that basement flat we had. You'd lie in bed at night and you'd hear noises. Some old man coming down the area steps to relieve himself. Women taking men on to the bomb-site next door. And screams. A lot of screams. You never found out afterwards what it had been.

Husband   You make a bit of money. You've a few pounds coming in. All you want is a little peace and quiet. You hire someone to keep an eye on things. Feed the dogs. Patrol the grounds. Keep out intruders. I said to him: 'You seem quiet enough.' He said: 'Ay, quiet enough.' And then you find him whispering to the dogs.

Wife   One night in January. Huddling round the oil-heater. The window was broken – some kids trying to get in. He sat there very quiet. Just staring into the heater. I didn't say anything. I could see he'd got an idea. I always know. That was the play about the couple who take in this blind beggar. You never discover his name. Slowly he takes over the house. He puts on the husband's clothes. He moves into bed with the wife. While the husband goes slowly blind as well.

Husband	I look out at night sometimes, after the house is locked up. I see him making his rounds in the dusk. Swinging his stick. Suddenly he'll hit out at a tree. Crack! I can't see what the expression is on his face.
Wife	Yes, and that play where the man who came to read the meter stayed and took over the house, and raped the wife, and kept the husband as a servant – he didn't think that up sitting in a garden.
Husband	And what happened last week, when the man called to read the meter? I'd given my man his instructions. I'd told him: 'Any meter-readers, that kind of thing, you stay with them and watch them until they're off the premises. Make sure the meter's the only thing they touch.' He stayed with him all right. They were in the stables looking at those meters for fifteen minutes or more. Talking together. What about?
Wife	Nor the one about the two men who came to the house claiming to be old school friends of the husband's. That was the one where the husband couldn't remember them, so they decide to share the wife between the three of them as a compromise. He thought of that while his brother was living with us. Thought of it on the area steps. There wasn't anywhere else to think.
Husband	He came to see me the other day. He said: 'There's a man at the gate says he may have known your wife in Streatham.' I said: 'There's very little I want in life. I want peace and quiet. That's all. Just peace and quiet. This is why I employ you. This is the reason for your presence in the lodge. This is why I spend the money I've earned on your services.' He said: 'This man's ill. He's dying. In the road.' I said: 'There are some leaves in the pool need getting out.' He looked at me then. Didn't say anything. Looked.
Wife	He could write his plays then! Oh yes! People coming to the door all the time, but it didn't seem to put him off. The rent collector. Old men from the spike. People to repossess the furniture. Men in white mackintoshes who said they'd known him years before in Stevenage. They'd walk about the rooms, putting their hands on our things, looking at my breasts. Never a moment's peace and quiet.

Husband Look at the way he walks. Slowly. Thoughtfully. No expression on his face. Touching things as he passes. Getting to know them. Putting a value on them. He looks at her like that. When I'm not there. I know. Looks at her breasts. Thinking, one day . . .

Pause.

Wife He's thought of something. About time. Now maybe we'll get a little peace and quiet.

Blots

Applicant   (*Thinks*) *Relax, relax, relax. They certainly won't take you if you seem nervous. They don't want neurotics for a job like this. Sit quite still. Look completely impassive. Don't think. Mind a blank . . . He spoke!*

(*Speaks*)   What?

(*Thinks*) *Did he speak?*

(*Speaks*)   Sorry . . . ? Giddiness? Do I suffer from giddiness? No.

What's he writing? It can't take him all that long to write 'no'. He's writing some comment on the way I said it.

                    What? Fits? No.

Don't just sit there snapping 'no' like that! Don't sound so defensive! He'll think there's something you're trying to hide. Be natural! Be conversational!

                    Blackouts? No, no, no. No blackouts. Never. Never. No, no, no.

That was dreadful. Did you see the way he looked at you? Be amused by it all! Sit back and enjoy it! Make jokes! Smile!

                    Psychiatric treatment? No, I've never had psychiatric treatment.

What's he driving at? Never mind – smile! Make conversation!

                    One of my aunts is rather eccentric. I mean, who can say exactly where the borderline is between eccentricity and madness? It must be established by the people around one, by the society in which one lives . . .

Keep going!

The place my aunt lives in is Matlock. It's in Derbyshire. Do you know Derbyshire at all? I *love* the Peak District. I love the countryside. I'm interested in . . . natural things. But no, I've never had psychiatric treatment.

Oh God! He thinks I'm crazy! Well, don't look crazy, then! Go on being amused!

Intrusive? These questions? Not at all! Anyway, I love intrusive questions! Intrude away!

No! No more laughs! Just smile! He thinks I'm insecure, doesn't he. He thinks I'm unstable. He'll start giving me mental tests next.

What? Look at what? What card? Where?

Ink blots! Oh my God, it's the ink blots! He's giving me the ink blots! I knew it!

What can I see? Well, that's a . . . It's a sort of . . . well . . . it looks like a kind of . . .

I musn't see any blood! I mustn't see any phallic symbols, or violence, or threatening clouds, or . . .

Two drunken men! It's two drunken men fighting, isn't it? No, no, no! I don't mean that!

No violence!

> I mean two women kissing each other.
> No, sorry! I'm just saying the first
> thing that comes into my head. But
> of course that's what you want me to
> do. Well, then, it's a man. It's a man
> standing with his legs apart – I mean
> a woman lying with her . . . No, no,
> no, I mean it's a man with a, well, a
> large kind of thing . . . No! No! No!
> Quick! What do I mean? I mean, it's
> a father hitting his child with an axe
> . . . I don't mean that at all. I mean it's
> a woman who's been split down the
> middle . . . This is absurd! These
> things are saying themselves!

Deep breath. Deep breath. Now, start all over again.

> Yes. Now I've got it. It's a sort of *calm*
> kind of scene. I mean, there's no
> conflict in it. There's no sex. There's
> no blood, or anything like that. It's
> a kind of natural scene . . . in the
> countryside . . . with grass and trees
> . . . and a thatched cottage . . .
> and cows . . . No! No cows! Oh, yes –
> cows . . . and so on . . .

*Why's he looking at me like that? He thinks I'm trying to
avoid conflict and sex. He thinks I'm repressing them.*

> I mean, there's a little sort of natural
> violence in the picture. The sort of
> violence you get in nature. I don't
> know – I think two of the cows are
> fighting. In a friendly way. And sex
> – there's some sex too. Once again I

see it as being somehow kind of natural. I think two of the cows . . . I mean a cow and a bull . . . Well, some of the birds . . .

Oh dear. Oh dear.

Go? Go where . . . ? Oh. You mean you've finished? But don't you want me to do any more tests . . . ? I suppose that means I've failed. Does it? You won't accept me for aircrew training? It's so unfair! I'm not neurotic normally! I'm only neurotic because I'm sitting here having questions fired at me! If I'd just been sitting here looking at that ink blot without people shouting at me and putting pressure on me I'd have thought it looked like something entirely different! Something more like a . . . I don't know – where's the card . . . ? Something more like . . . an A. It's a letter A! A G M T X Q R B . . . Hold on . . . This is an eye-test! Well, how am I supposed to see it's an eye-test if I haven't got my glasses on?

Through the Wilderness

Mother	It is nice now that all you boys have got cars of your own. You know how much it means to me when the three of you drive down to see me like this, and we can all have a good old chatter together.
John	That's right, Mother. So, as I was saying, Howard, I came down today through Wroxtead and Sudstow.
Howard	Really? I always come out through Dorris Hill and West Hatcham.
Ralph	I find I tend to turn off at the traffic lights in Manor Park Road myself and follow the 43 bus route through to the White Hart at Broylesden.
Mother	Ralph always was the adventurous one.
John	Last time I tried forking right just past the police station in Broylesden High Street. I wasn't very impressed with it as a route, though.
Howard	Weren't you? That's interesting. I've occasionally tried cutting through the Broylesden Heath Estate. Then you can either go along Mottram Road South or Creese End Broadway. I think it's handy to have the choice.
Ralph	Of course, much the prettiest way for my money is to carry on into Hangmore and go down past the pickles factory in Sunnydeep Lane.
Mother	Your father and I once saw Lloyd George going down Sunnydeep Lane in a *wheelbarrow* . . .
Howard	Did you, Mother? I'm not very keen on the Sunnydeep Lane way personally. I'm a great believer in turning up Hangmore Hill and going round by the pre-fabs on the Common.
Ralph	Yes, yes, there's something to be said for that too. What was the traffic like in Sudstow, then John?
John	Getting a bit sticky.
Howard	Yes, it was getting a bit sticky in Broylesden. How was it in Dorris Hill, Ralph?
Ralph	Sticky, pretty sticky.
Mother	The traffic's terrible round here now. There was a

	most frightful accident yesterday just outside when . . .
Howard	Oh, you're bound to get them in traffic like this.
Ralph	Where did you strike the traffic in Sudstow, then, John?
John	At the lights by the railway bridge. Do you know where I mean?
Ralph	Just by that dance hall where they had the trouble?
John	No, no. Next to the neon sign advertising mattresses.
Howard	Oh, you mean by the caravan depot? Just past Acme Motors?
John	Acme Motors? You're getting mixed up with Heaslam Road, Surley.
Howard	I'm pretty sure I'm not, you know.
John	I think you are, you know.
Howard	I don't think I am, you know.
John	Anyway, that's where I struck the traffic.
Ralph	I had a strange experience the other day.
John	Oh, really?
Ralph	I turned left at the lights in Broylesden High Street and cut down round the back of Coalpit Road. Thought I'd come out by the Wemblemore Palais. But what do you think happened? I came out by a new parade of shops, and I thought, hello, this must be Old Hangmore. Then I passed an Odeon –
John	An Odeon? In Old Hangmore?
Ralph	– and I thought, that's strange, there's no Odeon in Old Hangmore. Do you know where I was? In *New* Hangmore!
Howard	Getting lost in New Hangmore's nothing. I got lost last week in Upsome!
John	I went off somewhere into the blue only yesterday not a hundred yards from Sunnydeep Lane!
Mother	I remember I once got lost in the most curious circumstances in Singapore . . .
Ralph	Anybody could get lost in Singapore, Mother.
John	To become personal for a moment, Howard, how's your car?
Howard	Not so bad, thanks, not so bad. And yours?
John	Oh, not so bad, not so bad at all.
Mother	I had another of my turns last week.
Howard	We're talking about cars, mother, CARS.

Mother	Oh, I'm sorry.
John	To change the subject a bit – you know where Linden Green Lane comes out, just by Upsome Quadrant?
Howard	Where Tunstall Road joins the Crescent there?
Ralph	Just by the Nervous Diseases Hospital?
John	That's right. Where the new roundabout's being built.
Howard	Almost opposite a truss shop with a giant model of a rupture belt outside?
Ralph	Just before you get to the bus station?
Howard	By the zebra crossing there?
John	That's right. Well, I had a puncture there on Friday.
Ralph	Well, then, I suppose we ought to think about getting back.
Howard	I thought I might turn off by the paint factory on the by-pass this time and give the Apex roundabout a miss.
John	Have either of you tried taking that side road at Tillotsons' Corner?
Ralph	There's a lot to be said for both ways. A lot to be said.
Mother	I'll go and make the tea while you discuss it, then. I know you've got more important things to do than sit here listening to an old woman like me chattering away all afternoon.

Never Mind the Weather

Aunt Lil We've just been on our first cruise! Yes, our first one ever!
Oh, we had a lovely time! We're quite converted! Beautiful
boat, it was. Oh, an absolutely first-class boat. Not one
of those big luxury liners where you have to change for
dinner. We shouldn't fancy that. That's not our style.
No, a nice little boat. Well, about 300 cubits long. Made
of gopher wood, which I believe is very good for making
boats out of. And a nice homey atmosphere. In fact it was
more for cargo than passengers, really. Cattle, and pigs,
and sheep, and that type of thing. Oh, we're all very fond
of animals so it didn't worry us! The weather was a bit,
you know, *mixed*. But it didn't matter, you felt you were
seeing the world. Don't ask me where we went exactly
– we went all over the place! All round the Holy Land,
all round there. And we finished up by putting in at that
famous mountain they've got out there. What's it called?
Not Vesuvius. It'll come to me in a minute. We were
rather pleased to see it, actually! We'd had one or two days
quite bad weather, you see. Oh yes, it was quite bad at
times. But it didn't worry us. That's the wonderful thing
about a cruise. You don't have to go out. You've got all the
entertainment provided. So we didn't care if it rained all
the time. Well, you make your own fun, don't you? The
whole family was there, after all. Oh, yes! We all went! My
husband and I – his brother Shem and his wife – Ham
and his wife. And the boys brought their Mum and Dad!
Sweet! You should have seen us all! You'd have thought
we owned the ship! In fact, we were the only passengers.
So we had the run of it. Which was nice. Talk about fun
and games! Particularly when the weather was bad! Oh,
they all said the same thing, they all said they'd never seen
anything like it before. Half the time we really and truly
didn't know whether we were ever going to see land again.
I said to Dad, I said, 'At least the rats haven't deserted us!'
Because we had rats on board. Not many. You'd see one

or two from time to time. Yes, the storm lasted forty days, non-stop! They sent off a pigeon at one point, to see if it could get a message through. It was as bad as that. Still, it was a holiday, that's the main thing. And I took a lovely picture of the rainbow – I've got it here somewhere. Well, it's lovely of Japhet – the rainbow didn't come out.

Black and Silver

A hotel bedroom in Venice.

Night. **Husband** *and* **Wife** *are asleep. The window is open; reflections of lapping water move tranquilly up the wall outside. The curtain stirs in the night breeze. From somewhere in the distance there is a snatch of song. A church clock strikes three. It is followed by the sound of a small baby starting first to fret and then to cry. At the first serious cry the* **Wife** *starts up in bed, eyes still shut. She remains like that for a moment. The baby stops crying. The* **Wife**'s *head falls back on the pillow like a stone. A moment's silence, and then the baby starts to cry again. Once more the* **Wife** *sits up in bed. This time she rubs her eyes and opens them; drags her hands down over her face; licks her lips; runs a weary hand through her hair. She sighs, and braces herself with determination as if she is going to get up. Instead she drives her elbow into her* **Husband**'s *back.*

Wife   Your turn.

For a moment nothing happens. Then, in one complete delayed reflex action, the **Husband** *rolls straight out of bed on to his feet and heads for the door of the bathroom, his eyes still shut. His* **Wife** *falls back on the pillow, asleep.*

Husband   (*inarticulately, his voice muscles still anaesthetized by sleep*) All right! Just going! Leave it to me! Sh!

A chair carrying the clothes stands between him and the door. He falls over it noisily. The **Wife** *sits up in bed at once.*

Wife   (*whispering*) Sh! You'll wake the whole hotel!
Husband   (*blindly picking up himself and the chair, and piling the clothes back on to it*) Sh! Relax! Leave it all to me! You're supposed to be having a holiday, remember.

He moves the chair out of harm's way, then opens the bathroom door and pulls out a carry-cot on a conveyor, which he starts to push hurriedly back and forth. The crying stops and the **Wife** *subsides on to her pillow again. The* **Husband**, *whose eyes are still shut, and whose attitude suggests that he is trying to remain asleep on his feet, gradually ceases his pushing and creeps back to bed. When he gets to where the chair originally was, he stops and makes a careful detour, which brings him up against it in its new position. Once again he falls over it; the baby cries; the* **Wife** *starts up accusingly.*

Husband   (*putting the chair back into its original place, and returning to quiet the baby*) OK! Just going! Don't worry! Leave it to me! I'll fix it! Sh!

He pushes the carry-cot back and forth. The baby quietens.

Wife   If you're going to go crashing about like this all night, you'd better put him back in the bathroom.

He wheels the cot into the bathroom, and emerges closing the door behind him. He heads back for bed, elaborately avoiding the chair in every possible position.

Wife   He is properly covered up, isn't he?
Husband   (*reassuringly*) Yes . . .
Wife   You did check?
Husband   Yes, yes.

He gets back into bed and settles down. A pause. The **Wife** *is still sitting up, worrying.*

Wife   Has he got a window open in there?
Husband   (*reassuringly, from the depths of the pillow*) Mm! Mm!

A pause

Wife   There aren't any windows in the bathroom.
Husband   (*explaining without waking up*) Urm urmle urmurmurm . . .

Wife	What?
Husband	(*wearily, taking his head out of the pillows*) I said no, but there's a ventilator.

A pause.

Wife	Do you think he's getting enough vitamins?

*Sighing, the **Husband** sits up and turns on the light.*

I mean, he brings up all his feed. He must bring up all the vitamins, too musn't he?

*The **Husband** looks at his watch.*

Husband	(*pleadingly*) It's three o'clock!

Offended at the implied rebuke, she turns away from him and lies down.

We're supposed to be on holiday! We're supposed to be getting some rest and relaxation!

Wife	Rest and relaxation!
Husband	What?
Wife	How can I relax when everyone in the restaurant has to look the other way each time he brings his feed up?
Husband	The *Italians* are all right – *they* don't mind him bringing his feed up. The Signora – all the girls who do the rooms – they think he's *marvellous*. It's all these English honeymoon couples.

He turns the light out and lies down.

Wife	Well, it wasn't my idea, coming back to Venice and getting the room we spent our honeymoon in.
Husband	All they get at this hotel are honeymooners! I don't think they've ever seen a baby before, half of them!
Wife	I feel like a spectre at the feast, coming into the restaurant with the baby every morning.
Husband	The *Italians* seem to think children are quite natural. 'E,

bambolino! O, che bello ragazzo! Can I hold him? *Eccolo!
Bambolino, bambolino, bambolino!* Look – his little hands
and foots! I keep him, yes?

*His voice dies away. He has become aware that the baby is
crying again. They both lie there, neither making the first move.
Then the* **Wife** *sits up, sighing. At once the* **Husband** *sits up,
too – resignedly.*

All right! All right! I'm on duty.

He swings his legs out of bed. The **Wife** *lies down again.*

He's stopped.

*He swings his legs back into bed. Immediately the crying
starts again. He swings his legs out of bed, walks slowly and
aggrievedly towards the bathroom.*

If you're going to be worn out every day, I suppose on
holiday's a good as time as any . . .

*He has reached the bathroom door, and is just about
to open it, but realizes that the baby has stopped crying
again. He stands stock still for a moment, listening
intently. Then he turns on his heel, and heads back
towards the bed.*

The only thing that worries me is whether all this doesn't
rather make a fool of one – whether it doesn't . . .

The crying starts again. The **Husband** *freezes, and turns back
towards the bathroom. The crying stops. He waits a moment,
then heads back towards the bed.*

. . . weaken one's personality as . . .

*He stops and swings back towards the bathroom, thinking to get
a step ahead in the game. But the baby doesn't cry. He resumes
his trip back to bed.*

. . . as a father, in one's . . .

He gets into bed.

. . . relationship with the child . . .

The baby at once starts to cry. This time the **Husband** *does nothing, except let his head sink into his hands. The* **Wife** *sits up, exasperated, as if the* **Husband** *had never made any effort at all.*

Wife	Are you going, or shall I?
Husband	(*wearily, getting up again*) No, no, no! Go to sleep. My round! I'm in the chair!

He trails to the bathroom, and pulls the carry-cot out, jiggling it back and forth as he does so. The crying dies away. The **Wife** *subsides on to her pillow. Suddenly, he sniffs, and frowns. He stops pushing the cot back and forth; at which the baby starts to cry again; at which the* **Wife** *sits up in bed. The* **Husband** *doesn't notice her, however, because he is bending low over the cot, lifting the blanket within, and sniffing cautiously. He starts up hastily, whereupon the* **Wife** *lies down again and feigns immediate sleep. The* **Husband** *silently curses his luck, then, automatically pushing the cot back and forth to quiet the baby, looks round at her and speaks ingratiatingly.*

Darling . . . !

There is no response. He goes over to her, dragging the cot, and his ingratiating tone becomes more urgent.

It's big jobs.

There is still no response. He shakes her uncertainly, undecided between firmness and gallantry.

Well, that's damned funny, I must say. She was awake a moment ago.

The **Husband** *turns to the cot and starts to remove the nappy.*

It's not that I *mind* doing it. It's just that I don't know where she keeps the stuff . . .

To the baby, in the special upbeat weedling tones reserved for talking to babies.

Yes, it's old Dad who's on the job tonight, because lucky old Mum happens to be all tucked up in bed snoring her head off . . . ! Yes, she does . . . ! Oh, what a little stinky lad! What a little pooey-wooey . . . uggy puggy . . .

His increasing preoccupation with the difficulties of the operation makes his tone suddenly peremptory.

No, lie still! Lie *still*, blast you, or you'll get your feet in it!

He looks round desperately, holding the baby's feet.

Something to wipe you with . . .

There is plainly nothing in sight. The baby gurgles contentedly. The **Husband** *addresses it in his weedling voice.*

It's all right for *you* to laugh! Yes, it's all right for *you* to laugh! I said it's all right for *you* to laugh . . . !

He looks desperately round again, returning to his more usual irritated adult tones.

But what the flaming hell has she done with the Kleenex? I don't know where she keeps things, do I, boy?

Still holding the baby's feet up with one hand, he peers into the bathroom.

She hides them all away in some godforsaken place, so I have to hold your bottom up in the air with one hand . . .

He sees what he wants, high up inside the bathroom, and reaches off impossibly for it, still holding the baby's feet.

. . . and with the other . . . do my best to . . .

The sentence is completed by a cascading crash of falling objects, which makes the **Wife** *sit up and put the light on, and brings her jumping out of bed and running to intervene. She gazes into the bathroom at her* **Husband's** *efforts. He speaks defensively.*

Wife	Well, fancy putting the Kleenex up on the topmost shelf! For God's sake! The whole of Venice must be awake by now!
Husband	(*sarcastically*) Do you usually change the baby up on the top shelf!
Wife	(*fetching both Kleenex and a clean paper nappy from the wreckage in the bathroom*) Go back to bed. I'll finish this.
Husband	(*trying to keep her away from the cot*) No, no, no – I'll do it. You're supposed to be having a holiday.
Wife	Some holiday . . .
Husband	Anyway, I'm doing it. You go back to bed and get some sleep.
Wife	Sleep! I've forgotten what the word means! I wouldn't know it if I saw it! Come on, out of there.

She brushes him out of the way and finishes changing the baby.

Husband	(*watching aggrievedly*) I don't know why you're so eager all of a sudden.
Wife	(*weedling, to baby*) Was it a nasty terrible surprise seeing that horrible Daddy man changing your nappy? (*Fiercely, to* **Husband**) Because you make such a bloody meal of it!
Husband	*You* put the Kleenex out of reach!
Wife	(*weedlingly, to baby*) Is he keeping you awake, too, then, throwing all the jars of Nappisan and all the packets of Bickiepegs and all the little tins of Heinz strained spinach round the bathroom? (*Fiercely, to* **Husband**) I don't know why you're so eager all of a sudden, come to that.
Husband	Because I don't see why you should store up all the credit for changing his nappy when I've done all the dirty work already, that's why!
Wife	This is the third time I've been up tonight.
Husband	It's the third time I've been up.

Wife	I was up most of last night.
Husband	Who cleared up the mess in the Doge's Palace?
Wife	*(turning on him indignantly)* I like that! What about the St Mark's incident . . . ?
Husband	*(suddenly conciliating)* Oh, come on – let's not fight.

He sits down on the bed. The **Wife** *turns back to finish the baby, agreeing to be slightly mollified.*

We had a great fight on our honeymoon. I can remember standing looking out of that window at the canal and thinking our marriage was over. I can't remember what we were arguing about, though. What on earth *did* we argue about before *he* was born? What did we talk about? What did we think about? We must have been bored out of our minds . . . Do you remember that day we went out to Torcello and had a drink at the hotel where Hemingway used to stay? And you picked one of their geraniums and pinned it on my shirt . . . ?

She turns to him, smiling slightly, and hands him the soiled nappy. He looks at it tenderly, rather as if it were a geranium, and puts his hands around hers.

Wife	Put it down the lavatory for me, will you?
Husband	Oh . . . Right.

He takes it out to the bathroom. She is just bending over the cot again when a sudden thought strikes her.

Wife	Peter! Remember not to turn on the hot water!
Husband	*(off)* What?
Wife	The hot water!

A colossal thumping of air-locked plumbing fills the night. At once the baby starts to cry. The **Wife's** *head droops. She takes the baby out of the cot, wrapped up in its shawl, and gets back into bed with it, cradling it. It stops crying. She turns out the light. The* **Husband** *comes out of the bathroom drying his hands. He seizes the cot and pushes it out to the bathroom* *addressing a few encouraging words to the interior of the cot on the way.*

Husband   Straight off to sleep now! There's a good boy!

The **Wife** *dozes off. The* **Husband** *executes a cunning retreat from the bathroom, then stands outside the door and listens. He smiles at the silence, and begins to creep away. But before he has gone more than a step or two he stops, frowning. He goes back and listens again. He frowns anxiously. He bends closer to the door and listens more intently. Then he pulls the cot out of the bathroom and puts his ear right down on top of it. He turns appalled to his* **Wife***, and says in a terrible panic-stricken whisper.*

I think he's stopped breathing!

The **Wife** *at once wakes with a start, and, still carrying the baby, jumps out of bed and runs to join the* **Husband***. She bends over the cot to listen.*

I mean, I don't want to wake him up if he is
breathing . . .

Wife   (*urgently*) Hold this . . .

She hands the baby to the **Husband***, and pulls back the covers from the cot. She panics completely.*

Oh my God, he's not there!

Wife *and* **Husband** *stare at each other for an instant in horror. But at that moment the baby gives a cry, and they both become aware of its whereabouts. The* **Wife** *snatches it out of the* **Husband's** *arms, with a look at him which suggests that he was attempting to murder it. She hugs and kisses it and puts it back into the cot. Reaction to their shock makes them both furious.*

Stupid trick to play!

Husband   Well, it wasn't my fault!

Wife	Not breathing!
Husband	Well, he *wasn't* breathing there – he was breathing somewhere else!

They both get grumpily back into bed. The **Wife** *has pulled the cot up to her side of the bed, so that she can keep jiggling it back and forth as she lies there. The* **Husband** *remains sitting up in bed with his arms round his knees.*

Well, I'm awake now. I couldn't go to sleep if you paid me . . .

There is no response from the **Wife**.

You realize it's not breakfast time for another five hours yet? You didn't pack any jigsaw puzzles, did you?

No response. A faint rhythmic squeaking of springs becomes audible.

	What's that?
Wife	What?
Husband	That squeak, squeak, squeak.

The **Wife** *stops pushing the cot to and fro for a moment and listens.*

Wife   Oh, that's the couple next door.

The **Husband** *frowns, puzzled. The light dawns.*

Husband   You mean, they've got a baby in there too? Pushing it back and forth like us?

The **Wife** *just looks at him.*

I thought they were all honeymoon couples in the hotel, apart from us.

The **Wife** *goes on staring.*

	Oh . . .! But at three o'clock in the morning?
Wife	We probably woke them up. Anyway, why not?
Husband	Well . . .!

He thinks.

	I suppose we used to make love in the middle of the night, sometimes. Didn't we? I can't remember. It all seems so long ago.
Wife	I can't remember what it was like at all before he was born.
Husband	What did we do with all that time?
Wife	We used to go to the cinema. Didn't we? Twice a week sometimes.
Husband	We went out for meals in Chinese restaurants.
Wife	We stayed in bed on Sundays . . .

The squeaking has ceased. The **Wife** *stops jiggling the cot and turns to the* **Husband**.

| | Oh, Peter! What's happened to us? Have we changed? Have I changed? I have, haven't I? |
| **Husband** | (*reassuringly*) No, you haven't. |

He puts his arm round her.

| **Wife** | Do you still love me? |
| **Husband** | Of course I do. |

He squeezes her affectionately.

Wife	But not just out of habit? Not just out of a sense of duty?
Husband	(*stroking her head*) No!
Wife	I still . . . you know . . . *attract* you?

He kisses her mouth, and silences her.

Even though I'm so preoccupied with him . . .?

He kisses her again.

. . . and so ill-tempered and . . . ?

He kisses her again, pressing her back on to the pillow.

. . . so on?

She gazes up at him in silence.

We'll have to be very quiet, then . . .

Just as he is about to kiss her again, the baby starts to fret. They both freeze. The **Husband** *looks round murderously at the cot.*

Oh . . . Never mind! Go on!

The **Husband** *continues to stare at the cot. The baby falls silent again. Slowly the* **Husband** *turns back to kiss his* **Wife**. *She puts her arm around him. Once again the baby begins to cry. Once again the* **Husband** *looks round desperately. Without letting go of the* **Husband**, *the* **Wife** *stretches out her arm and begins to push the cot back and forth. The crying stops. Still pushing, she tries to encourage her* **Husband**.

I love you!

Husband	(*doing his best to concentrate on her*) I love you!
Wife	Go on then! Don't stop!

But he turns to look at the cot, then disengages himself from her and sits up gloomily.

Husband   I'll wait till you've got him back to sleep again.

He lies back against the pillows beside her. She sighs, and takes his hand.

Wife   I'm sorry, love . . . I'm sorry. I feel it's all my fault.

They lie side by side, gazing in front of them, hand in hand, she pushing the cot back and forth. Gradually the **Husband**'s *head begins to loll, and his eyes close.*

Do you remember that day right at the end of the honeymoon, when we came back across the Lagoon in the twilight in that man's old motorboat, and the water was absolutely still – all black and silver, black and silver – and we dropped anchor and swam and the water was so warm and dark that you felt you could just let yourself go, and drift down into it forever . . . ?

She turns and sees that his eyes are shut.

You're not going to sleep? Are you?

His head slips a little further sideways.

I thought we were going to . . . Peter!

She prods him sharply. There is a momentary pause, and then, in one complete delayed reflex action, he rolls straight out of bed on to his feet, as at the beginning, and heads for where the cot was, his eyes still shut.

Husband (*inarticulately*) All right! Just going! Sh! Leave it to me . . . !

Blackout, as he once again falls over the chair, and the baby cries.

The New Quixote

*The living-room of Gina's tiny one-up one-down urban
cottage. Once, presumably, it housed a tiny artisan and his tiny
wife and ten tiny children. Now, from its decoration and fur-
nishing, it houses a single lady with taste, professional salary,
and firmly-set neat ways. A front door opens direct from the
street; another door gives access to the stairs and everything else.*

*The room is empty, and half-dark, the only light coming
around the drawn curtains at the window. Somewhere church
bells are ringing.*

The stairs door opens, and **Gina** *enters, yawning and
pulling a dressing-gown over her nightdress. She draws the
curtains, blinking in the light, and looks at her watch.*

Gina   Quarter to eleven . . . Oh God! – Sundays!

*She goes to the front door, takes in a Sunday paper and a
single pint of milk, and crosses towards the stairs door.*

Waste, waste, waste, waste, waste . . .

*She stops just as she is about to go out, realising that she has
seen something out of place. She puts down the papers and the
milk, and goes back to pick up a drab-coloured plastic mac lying
across one of the armchairs. She stares at it, puzzled, then sees
that lying beneath it is a small, shabby, brown rucksack. She
picks this up, too. The flap is open. She pulls out a thermos
flask, a couple of heavy reference books, and a slide rule.
She stares at the objects, then round the room, baffled. Then
suddenly she remembers. She catches her breath and claps a
hand to her mouth, then laughs guiltily at herself.*

Oh, dear! Oh, Lordy! Forgotten all about him!

*Giggling guiltily, she goes to the stairs door and calls rather
uncertainly.*

Um . . hello . . . ! Are you still here, then . . . ? Are you in the bathroom, um. . . ?

She looks inside the flap of the rucksack.

. . . K. B. Prosser Esquire? Keith?

No reply. She closes the door, and stand there thoughtfully.

Or was it Kenneth? He had a van, didn't he?

She goes to the front door, and looks out.

Gone . . . Oh, dear! Never just forgotten all about it before. That really is beginning to get a bit sleazy.

She gives herself a very small laugh, more shocked at herself than she would like to admit. She turns it into a joke, and smacks her hand.

Smack, smack, smack! If it happens again – the headmistress!

She looks at the raincoat and rucksack.

I'd better post them on – I don't suppose he'll feel much like coming back for them now . . . Brown paper, while I think of it . . .

She goes out through the stairs door, closing it behind her. At once a key turns in the front door, and **Kenneth** *enters. He is in his twenties, and is wearing spectacles, an open-necked shirt, a shapeless sports jacket with a row of pens in the breast-pocket, and brown corduroy trousers. From his appearance you suspect at once that he collects train numbers, or plays chess, or is a radio ham. He is in fact carrying a load of electronic equipment – the uncased elements of a home-made stereophonic rig. He spreads them over the neat period furniture and plugs them in. Then he goes quietly across to the stairs door and listens. Reassured by the silence, he walks lightly back to the front door, and carries in a couple of loudspeakers and an*

*armful of records. He connects up the loudspeakers and puts
on a record. The room is at once filled with Messiaen, played
at full stereo enthusiast's loudness. He opens the stairs door to
let the sound out in that direction, then goes out of the front
door again, very pleased with himself.* **Gina** *comes running
in through the stairs door, astonished and terrified. She gazes
round the room with incomprehension, covers her ears, and
runs to the control panel, trying to find some way of turning it
off.* **Kenneth** *comes in through the front door, carrying
another load of records and books. At the sight of* **Gina**
*he puts them down and runs to embrace her. She backs
away, appalled. They shout to each other inaudibly over
the noise.*

Kenneth	Darling!
Gina	What? What is all this?
Kenneth	I thought I'd give you a surprise! An aubade!
Gina	What?
Kenneth	A morning song!
Gina	What?

She gestures to him to turn the sound down. He does so.

Kenneth	To serenade you awake! Like Wagner playing the Siegfried Idyll to Cosima!
Gina	Well, listen, Keith . . .
Kenneth	Kenneth.
Gina	I mean Kenneth.
Kenneth	'Keith!'

*Laughing at her mistake, he kisses her again. As he does so,
he stretches out a hand and turns up the gramophone full
blast again.*

Kenneth	(*shouting*) It's so fantastically sensual!
Gina	(*shouting*) Look, what is all this? What's going on?
Kenneth	(*shouting*) It's Messiaen! Messiaen!

He turns the sound down.

Messiaen! Turangalila, by Messiaen!

Gina	What?
Kenneth	We were talking about it last night. At the party. When we were sitting on the stairs. You remember! You just suddenly said how you liked Messiaen.
Gina	Did I?
Kenneth	I couldn't believe my ears! To meet someone like you who knew about Messiaen! I thought I couldn't have heard right over the noise! I just kept saying 'You like Messiaen?'
Gina	And what did I say?
Kenneth	You just . . . nodded and smiled . . .
Gina	Oh. That was the bit when I was nodding and smiling?
Kenneth	You kept nodding and smiling all the time! Oh, Gina! Supposing we hadn't met! Supposing you'd just decided to have an early night instead of going to the party!
Gina	Yes . . .
Kenneth	You'd be sitting here. I'd be sitting in my little room . . .
Gina	I thought you *had* gone, as a matter of fact.
Kenneth	Gone? Gone where?
Gina	Well, back to your . . . little room, or whatever.

He laughs at her tenderly, and kisses her.

Kenneth	Oh, you silly girl! I just went to fetch my stuff!

He goes out of the front door.

Gina	Your stuff? 'What stuff?'

He reappears with a suitcase and a couple of suits on hangers.

Kenneth	It didn't take long in the van. I don't believe in loading myself with a lot of personal possessions.

He goes out again.

Gina	Before you fetch anything else in, Keith . . .

He reappears carrying a number of pictures, and a polythene bag full of washing, smiling at her mistake.

Kenneth	Kenneth!

He shuts the front door.

That's the lot. Wherever my stereo and records are – that's home.

Gina	Kenneth, I think we'd better sit down quietly and have a serious talk.
Kenneth	I just want to talk and talk all day!

They sit down.

I've got so many things I must tell you! Oh, Gina!

Gina	Now, Kenneth . . .
Kenneth	You can call me Keith if you want to. I don't feel like Kenneth any more! I feel completely changed! As if I was walking about in a story, and it was all written down already! Do you know what I mean! It's like seeing the world for the first time! That chair, for instance – it's *beautiful!*
Gina	That chair? I should think it was – I paid £60 for it. Now listen, Kenneth, I don't want you to think I regret last night, or that I didn't enjoy it . . .
Kenneth	I never guessed what it could be like! I've only known girls of my own age before!
Gina	Well, that's another thing . . .
Kenneth	I didn't get to sleep at all! I couldn't believe it had happened! When it started to get light I got up and sat by the window for an hour, just looking out. Cars standing waiting all down the street. Covered with dew – dew all over their windscreens, as if their eyes were shut. Everything still. Just so. Just right. All written down already. Then I came and sat on the floor next to the bed, and looked at you. You were lying on your side, with your hair all over the pillow.

Instinctively she puts her hand up to it.

Every time you breathed out, it stirred the down at the corner of your mouth. You've got a faint, faint moustache – I hadn't realised.

She puts her hand over her upper lip.

No – I love it! I stroked it. Didn't you feel it in your sleep? I kissed the wrinkles at the corner of your eye.

She gets up and goes over to the window.

Gina	I'm very sorry about them.
Kenneth	I felt I wanted to cry.
Gina	About the wrinkles?
Kenneth	About you. Or about me. I knew all the first part of my life was over, all the silly bit. Now the serious part was starting.
Gina	Oh, dear!
Kenneth	Anyway, I decided to go and get my stuff, and move in properly before you woke up. I just quickly got dressed, and took the door key out of your bag. Mum was waiting in the hall when I came in – I've been living at home, you see. She said: 'Where have you been, Kenneth?' 'Oh – a friend's house.'

He laughs at the inadequacy of this formula. **Gina** *gazes at him uneasily.*

So I put the stuff in the van, and she said, 'Where are you going, then, Kenneth?' And I said, 'Oh – moving in with my friend.' And she said, 'Aren't you going to have some breakfast before you go?' And I said, 'No – I'll have breakfast there.' And that was that. All that part of my life – finished.

Gina	(*dismayed*) Oh, my dear sweet boy! What have you done?
Kenneth	And all the way back I thought, 'Now I can do anything! Nothing can touch me now!' And I drove on the wrong side of the road, and went into a roundabout at forty! I must have been mad! I couldn't steer! The back of the van skidded round and crashed into the wall! Then I thought, 'Oh God, I'm going to get killed before I can tell her about everything!' Because I wanted to tell you about the cars with dew on the windscreen, and about how I used to cycle to school, and how you looked when

you were asleep, and . . . and how the world is really completely different from what you think, and how everything's going to be all right. I wanted to say it all at once, in a great shout, but I couldn't think of the words. So I thought, I'll just creep in with the stereo, and I'll say *this* . . .

He turns up the Messiaen full blast. The he takes her hand and sits on the floor in front of her, gazing up at her. She laughs, touched in spite of herself. Then she gestures for the sound to be turned down. He does so.

Gina	Well, now you've said it.
Kenneth	Yes.
Gina	And I feel . . . very touched. But now let's just be serious for a moment, shall we?

He begins to pace up and down excitedly.

Kenneth I haven't even begun to tell you how I *feel* about everything! It's so complicated and surprising! I think what I feel most of all is . . .

He stops to examine his feelings.

Completely exhausted!

He slumps into the sofa, almost as if he is going to faint. She gazes at him.

Gina	I'll make you some breakfast.
Kenneth	(*palely, without rising*) I'll do it. You sit down.

She laughs and goes out through the stairs door.

Gina (*off*) Toast and coffee and orange-juice all right?

He nods, and stretches himself out full-length.

What?

Kenneth   (*faintly*) Yes, fine . . . Oh, dear! Oh dear oh dear . . . !

He closes his eyes and falls instantly asleep. **Gina** *re-enters carrying two glasses of orange-juice.*

Gina   Now, drink this up and you'll feel a lot better.

She sits down on the edge of the sofa, and sets his orange-juice down on the floor beside him.

Now, Kenneth, be a good boy and listen to what I'm going to say very carefully, and don't misunderstand me. I like you very much, Kenneth, and I hope we shall see quite a lot of each other. But I don't think we ought to rush our fences. I'm a lot older than you . . .

He snorts in his sleep.

Well, I am. You're very young and impulsive – full of enthusiasm for life . . .

He snores. She looks round at him.

Oh, *no!* Oh, *Lord!* If you can't hear what's been said at parties, never, never, never nod and smile!

She gets up and picks up the record sleeve.

Messiaen . . . ! I might have guessed it would be something like that we were talking about.

She looks down at him.

What was I like at that age? I didn't go around behaving like this!

She bends close to examine his face, frowning. She feels his upper lip, then her own. She feels the corners of his eyes, and then the corners of her own eyes.

It won't do, will it? Look at all this stuff! Picasso prints!

Oh, heavens! A bag of dirty washing! That's for me, I suppose.

In a funny voice.

'It's no good – he'll have to go.'

She turns up the Messiaen full blast. He stirs, half-opens his eyes, and smiles at her. She turns the sound down again, and sits down on the edge of the sofa.

	Are you properly awake?
Kenneth	Um.

He sits up and puts his arms round her, and pulls her down on top of him. She struggles free.

Gina	No, no, no! We've got to be serious for a moment. Have a drink of orange-juice and clear your head.

She hands him the glass. He drinks, dazed.

	One thing we must get straight at once, Kenneth. You can't stay here.
Kenneth	Oh, sorry, Gina. I'll move upstairs into the bed.
Gina	No, I mean you can't just *move in* like this!
Kenneth	(*baffled*) Why not?
Gina	Well, because . . . because you can't! I haven't invited you to, have I?
Kenneth	How long have I been asleep? What's been happening? When I went to sleep everything was new and different. I wake up and it's all back to normal again.
Gina	I'm sorry, Kenneth.
Kenneth	We love each other, don't we?
Gina	Well . . .
Kenneth	I love you. You love me. Don't you?
Gina	Well . . .
Kenneth	Of course you do, Gina! You said you did, last night.
Gina	Did I?

Kenneth	Yes!
Gina	On the stairs, was this? Nodding and smiling?
Kenneth	In bed!
Gina	Oh . . . *then* . . .
Kenneth	Yes, then!
Gina	But supposing somebody comes in?
Kenneth	Who?
Gina	Well, a friend . . .
Kenneth	That's all right. I shan't be embarrassed . . . What sort of friend?
Gina	Well, let's say a man. Someone coming to take me out.
Kenneth	(*staring at her*) You've got men who . . . take you out?
Gina	Well, yes. I'm not that old, am I?
Kenneth	You never told me that.
Gina	You never asked.
Kenneth	But you wouldn't let them . . . take you out *now*.
Gina	How do you mean, *now*?
Kenneth	I mean, after . . . well, *now*.
Gina	What do you want me to do, Kenneth? Ring them all up and tell them not to call?
Kenneth	How many of them are there?
Gina	Well, I don't know – I don't keep a list . . .
Kenneth	But there are several!
Gina	Yes!
Kenneth	Not just one special one?
Gina	No! Well . . . yes.
Kenneth	There *is* a special one?
Gina	Yes.
Kenneth	Someone you used to be in love with?
Gina	*Used* to be in love with?
Kenneth	Before.
Gina	Well . . . someone I'm . . . fond of.
Kenneth	But not in love with?
Gina	Look, he's someone I've known for a long time. I don't want to hurt his feelings. He'll be very upset if he comes in through that door and finds you and all your stuff in occupation.
Kenneth	He's not coming today, is he?
Gina	Well, he may!
Kenneth	Oh, God – I should never have gone to sleep!

Gina	As a matter of fact he is. He's coming to take me out to lunch.
Kenneth	You must explain to him, then, love!
Gina	Now, Kenneth, be a good boy . . .
Kenneth	*I'll* explain to him!
Gina	Oh, Kenneth! We'll see each other next week some time.
Kenneth	What sort of man is he? Older than me?
Gina	Yes.
Kenneth	Is he . . . handsome?
Gina	Yes.
Kenneth	What kind of work does he do?
Gina	He . . . works for one of those big oil companies.
Kenneth	What's his name?
Gina	Lionel.
Kenneth	Lionel . . . Where's he taking you for lunch?
Gina	I don't know!
Kenneth	What sort of places does he usually take you to? Expensive places?
Gina	Sometimes.
Kenneth	The Ritz? The Dorchester? Places like that?
Gina	More or less.
Kenneth	Night clubs?
Gina	Occasionally.

He continues to stare at her. Then suddenly he laughs and relaxes.

Kenneth	Oh, Gina, darling! For a moment I thought you were being serious!

He kisses her. She gazes at him in astonishment.

	I'm going to get the breakfast. I'm starving.
Gina	Kenneth . . .
Kenneth	No, no – you sit down. You must be tired, too. I'm very good in the kitchen. Tomorrow I'll bring you breakfast in bed.

Solicitously he turns up the Messiaen full blast, blows her another kiss, and goes out through the stairs door. She gazes after him in astonishment.

Gina   (*shouting*) I am being serious! Oh, damn this noise!

She turns down the gramophone.

I am serious! Why do you think I'm not?

He reappears in the doorway, holding the butter-knife.

Kenneth   (*with amused gentleness*) Women don't fall in love with handsome men who take them to night clubs! Where's the butter?

Gina   (*bemused*) In the cupboard over the sink.

He disappears again.

Don't they?

He reappears, holding the butter.

Kenneth   Well, some women may. But *you* don't, Gina, love, you silly girl!

He kisses her neck.

You fall in love with scruffy, short-sighted men like me, who work for obscure electronics firms, and arrive with all their dirty washing in a plastic bag. Sit down, darling . . .

She sits down, unable to think of a reply. He goes out of the door again.

Gina   What we've got to bear in mind, Kenneth, is Lionel's feelings. We have known each other a very long time, you see. He's very jealous. When he comes in and sees you . . . and all this dirty washing, and so on . . . he'll go crazy, he really will.

Kenneth *enters, holding the coffee-pot.*

Kenneth	I really don't think he cares for you very much, Gina.
Gina	How do you know? You haven't met him!
Kenneth	If he really cared for you he wouldn't have to fling himself about in jealous rages, would he? I'm not flinging myself about in a jealous rage. He's just trying to prove to himself that he really loves you. That's why he takes you to all those night clubs and places! The more demonstrative someone is, the more he's trying to cover up for his real lack of feeling underneath.
Gina	He may hit you, or something.
Kenneth	Exactly!
Gina	He may . . . break your gramophone!
Kenneth	I shan't let him do that, I'm afraid. I built that stereo myself.
Gina	You may not be able to stop him! He's very . . . powerfully built.
Kenneth	The tougher they look on the surface, the softer they are underneath. Where's the sugar?
Gina	Same place as the butter.

He goes out again.

The softer they look on the surface, the tougher they are to get rid of.

He reappears, carrying coffee and toast for them both on a tray.

Kenneth	I can find my way round your kitchen without any trouble at all.
Gina	So I see.
Kenneth	Sit down, love.

She sits, reluctantly, then attempts to pour the coffee.

No, no, I'll do it! White? I like being in your kitchen. Lots of dark red flowery things. All the white bits just the right shade of white – not too clinical. Everything quietly in its place. Everything just so . . . I have tried living with a girl once before, as a matter of fact.

Gina   Really? Was she surprised?

Kenneth   It was terrible. She shared the flat with two other girls. They all used to wash their hair in the kitchen sink. They dried their stockings over the breakfast table.

She sighs.

Tired?

Gina   A little weary, in some ways.

Kenneth   Like some music?

Gina   No, no, no.

Kenneth   I know – I'll feed you.

He kneels up in front of her and tries to feed her buttered toast. She waves it away.

No?

Gina   I don't think I'm hungry after all.

Kenneth   I'm not sure I am, either. I feel so strange! Disembodied! As if today it was a completely different world, where there were just words, and feelings, and no one's feet quite touched the ground . . . I went all over the house during the night, when I couldn't sleep. Did you hear me? Do you know that I was doing? I was smelling everywhere.

Gina   You remind me of someone. I wish I could think who.

Kenneth   I smelt you. I smelt your clothes. Then I went and smelt the bathroom. You can always tell what someone's like by the smell of the bathroom. Don't you think so?

Gina   What am I like, then?

Kenneth   I can't say it – I can only smell it. The whole house smelt good, Gina. Neat, tidy. You could smell the clock ticking.

Gina   You do remind me of someone. Perhaps it's someone I saw in a dream.

Kenneth   I know why you told me all that stuff about Lionel. I know why you were trying to get rid of me.

Gina   What? I wasn't trying to get rid of you, exactly. I was just trying to . . .

Kenneth	You just suddenly felt you couldn't stand the sight of me another minute.
Gina	No, no . . .
Kenneth	Don't worry! I know how it is sometimes. You get afraid of your own feelings. They seem so huge and uncontrollable – you don't know where they're going to take you. In a way, the stronger your feelings are, the more you want to deny them. Every time I look at you and see No, no, no! in your eyes – oh, I'm not blind, I can see it there sometimes! – every time I see you looking No, no, no! I realise it actually means Yes, yes, yes!
Gina	I see.
Kenneth	(*smiling tenderly*) You're doing it now!
Gina	Oh am I? Really?

She turns her eyes away from him, confused.

Kenneth	Don't worry! I know what you really mean!

He kisses her hand.

Gina	This idea you've got that everything's the opposite of what it seems . . .
Kenneth	Yes!
Gina	You seem to be rather taken with it.
Kenneth	Yes, I am!
Gina	Are you sure you've got it right?
Kenneth	It sounds crazy, doesn't it?

He laughs.

	But as a matter of fact it's my . . . sort of . . . philosophy of life. Don't laugh about it! We shouldn't have met each other without it!
Gina	Shouldn't we?
Kenneth	I got to the party last night, and saw you almost as soon as I came through the door. You were standing on the other side of the room, talking to someone, smiling slightly . . . You looked so self-contained and unapproachable!

Gina	So you approached?
Kenneth	Yes! I knew you were looking like that just to protect yourself, because you were really very sweet and soft-hearted and vulnerable. It's taken me years to work it out! All the girls I met at parties always seemed to keep smiling distantly and shaking their heads and looking over my shoulder at somebody else. I thought there was something wrong with *me*! I didn't realise that every time they yawned they were really saying yes!
Gina	How do you say no, then?
Kenneth	By saying yes! That's what they all thought *I* was doing when I tried to grab their hands, and asked if I could take them home afterwards!
Gina	(*faintly*) More coffee?
Kenneth	(*his mind still on the girls*) Yes, please.

She goes to pour it, uncertainly. He does not pay any attention to her.

I mean, no thanks.

She pours it, and he accepts it absent-mindedly.

Then I started reading Freud. It was like a revelation! Whatever you seem to be on the surface, it's because you're trying to surpress the opposite inside! You're trying not to admit the inadmissible! You're overcompensating! Well, then it all fell into place! All the books I'd read! All the plays I'd seen! What's the whole of modern literature about, from beginning to end? It's about how everything's not what it seems to be! You start with someone who seems to be a hero – and it turns out in the end that he was really a coward all the time. He looks respectable – he turns out to be a criminal. Looks happy – turns out to be miserable. The sane insane – the insane saner than the sane. If it's bad it's good, and if it's good it's bad. It's all obvious as soon as you see it!

Gina	So now you go to parties and look for hard-faced women with scornful smiles . . . ?
Kenneth	Yes! And instead of saying, 'When can I see you again?' I

just stand there looking helpless and saying I haven't got a
bed for the night.

Gina   And at once they sense the hidden masculinity?

Kenneth   Well, people like to work things out for themselves,
don't they!

Gina   (*wryly*) I suppose they like to have new personalities
discovered inside them, too.

Kenneth   Yes, they do.

Gina   It always works, does it?

Kenneth   Well, last night was the first time, really. But crumbs!
What a first time!

*He kisses her enthusiastically, and begins to pace up and down
the room.*

But it's not just people, you see, Gina. It's everything! It's
a general theory for understanding the whole universe!
You look at this, and you think, this is a chair. But you
look into it more closely and you'll see it's not a chair at
all. It's a mass of tiny spinning particles! And what about
the particles! Are they really and truly particles? Of course
not – they're not particles at all! They're electricity!
They're energy! Matter is energy!

Gina   (*gently*) You're a nut, on top of everything else. Aren't you!
A real full-blown nut.

Kenneth   The nuttier it all seems, the more reasonable it actually
is. Look at this piece of empty air in front of us. Well,
of course, it's not empty. It's a mixture of nitrogen and
oxygen, with a proportion of water vapour and carbon
dioxide, and traces of argon, neon, helium, krypton and
xenon. It's also polluted with industrial emission gases.
It's laden with pollen. It's alive with bacteria. It's full of
voices and music from radio stations! Voices speaking
high and low; shouting, muttering, singing, sobbing,
talking Swahili, Lithuanian, Berber, Welsh, Dutch, Malay!
It's crossed by cosmic rays from space; by rays of light
from Arcturus, Betelgeuse, and the Crab Nebula; and by
faint, faint radio waves from galaxies receding almost at
the speed of light on the very edge of the universe! All
here, in this piece of empty air between the two of us!

Gina	(*tenderly*) But you look so sweet, with the light flashing on your specatacles like that . . .
Kenneth	What?
Gina	Are you really all hard and grown-up underneath?
Kenneth	Well, I think in a crisis . . . You can see from books and plays that it takes a crisis to bring out the truth. If you went through life without a crisis you might never find out what anything was like at all.
Gina	And your collar open, and your arms waving about . . .
Kenneth	But the thing is, Gina, the implications of all this! Because, you see, if right's wrong, and bad's good, and energy's matter, and a chair isn't a chair – then the whole structure of logic collapses! The whole of mathematics! The very possibility of organised thought . . . !

He stops in mid-stride, suddenly realising that she is crying.

Gina! What's the matter?

He runs to comfort her.

Gina	Oh, sweetest! Never mind! Logic and mathematics don't matter all that much! We'll get by without them! We've got on all right up to now! Perhaps I was exaggerating a bit, anyway. It might be possible to think some thoughts. I've just suddenly remembered who it is you remind me of. It *was* someone in a dream. I dreamt once I had a son. He was grown-up already in my dream – he was a young man. And he walked up and down, with the neck of his shirt open, full of ideas, so bright and quick and excited by everything . . .
Kenneth	It proves I'm right, though, doesn't it! There we were yesterday with you self-possessed and me helpless and here we are today with you in tears and me comforting you.
Gina	Unless I made the whole dream up when I saw you . . .
Kenneth	My moving in – that was the crisis. I told you you had to have a crisis, didn't I!
Gina	I don't suppose I shall ever have a son now. My life hasn't turned out like that.

Kenneth	Don't be sad. I'll look after you. I'll cook the dinner and bring you breakfast in bed.
Gina	(*stroking his head*) Poor old Kenneth!
Kenneth	No, poor old Gina!
Gina	Me weeping on your shoulder like this.
Kenneth	I knew you would. I knew as soon as I saw you.
Gina	You poor boy! You sweet boy! You sweet poor kind boy!
Kenneth	Don't worry about your friend Lionel. I'll deal with him. Have him crying on my other shoulder in no time.
Gina	There isn't any Lionel. There isn't anyone coming.
Kenneth	You made him up?
Gina	Sort of.
Kenneth	I knew there was something wrong with him!
Gina	There's no one I'm really fond of.
Kenneth	I told you, didn't I? As soon as you started saying he was powerfully built, and very demonstrative, and so on. I said at once, 'There's something he's trying to cover up.'
Gina	I felt I had to get you out of here.
Kenneth	I know you did.
Gina	All your stuff . . . I felt almost hysterical!
Kenneth	The more hysterical you got, the more I knew what you really felt.
Gina	You knew?
Kenneth	Yes.
Gina	All the time?
Kenneth	Yes.
Gina	I didn't know!
Kenneth	I know you didn't.
Gina	I really thought I wanted you to go! I thought you were intolerable!
Kenneth	(*smiling*) Yes.
Gina	Bumptious, half-baked . . .
Kenneth	Crack-brained, unfeeling . . .
Gina	That's what I thought. Or that's what I thought I thought.
Kenneth	Yes, whatever you're thinking, it's never what you think you're thinking.
Gina	No, I see that now. I was feeling what I seemed to be feeling just to stop myself feeling what I didn't know I was feeling.
Kenneth	It's as simple as that.

| Gina | It was only when I saw you walking up and down . . . waving your arms about . . . so excited . . . like a little boy . . . |

She starts to cry again.

| Kenneth | Sh! Oh, Gina, this has been the most wonderful day of my life. I can't tell you what it's like, suddenly having all your ideas proved like this! It doesn't usually work out so neatly. I've spent weeks and months with unapproachable girls sometimes, trying to get through. Knowing it was there underneath. But finding it was buried so deep you could never get through . . . |

She strokes his head.

	But you just have to have faith. You just have to go on and try again. I got knocked unconscious once.
Gina	By a girl?
Kenneth	By a man. Outside a pub. He kept grabbing hold of people and shouting 'Want a fight, then?' I knew he was really a coward. So I went up to him, and looked him straight in the eye, and he hit me in the stomach.
Gina	Oh, poor love!
Kenneth	Well, it proved my point, of course. But I cracked my head on the edge of the pavement. Had to have five stitches.
Gina	Well, I'm going to look after you, and everything's going to be different. I shan't let anyone yawn at you, or hit you in the stomach.
Kenneth	That's the terrible thing, *knowing you're right* when everyone else can plainly see you're wrong!
Gina	I'm going to feed you up. You're so thin! What was she giving you, that mother of yours? We'll have a proper Sunday lunch for a start.

She kisses him, and goes to the bag of washing.

Now where's all this washing that needs to be done?

Kenneth	*Knowing you're right*, when everything around you definitely proves you're wrong! That's the terrible thing!
Gina	Do you like a little starch in your collars? Oh dear, button off here . . .
Kenneth	Well, it's the marvellous thing, really. Because that's how you know you're right! The whole history of the world has been made up of people who were *obviously wrong*, who turned out in the end to be right!
Gina	Some of these pants seem a bit saggy round the waist.
Kenneth	It's when something's obviously right that you have to start worrying! When people start taking you seriously! When everything seems to fit!
Gina	Shall I see if I can put some new elastic in for you?

He does not answer, lost in thought. She goes to him and kneels beside him.

What a dreamy boy! Look at him!

He turns and smiles at her abstractedly.

We're an odd pair, aren't we? Do you think it will be all right?

Kenneth	(*abstractedly*) Yes.
Gina	I can imagine what people will say . . . You won't mind?
Kenneth	No, no . . .
Gina	Perhaps it's all right. Perhaps it's just what you've been saying – we're so ill-matched that it *must* be all right!
Kenneth	Yes.
Gina	Oh, I'm so happy! Are you?
Kenneth	Yes.
Gina	What are you thinking about?
Kenneth	Oh, nothing.
Gina	You're not worrying about something?

He sighs.

You musn't worry your head about anything now. That's all over.

Kenneth	I was just thinking.

Gina	Why don't you have a little rest from thinking?
Kenneth	I was just thinking about us, as the days go by, sitting here having breakfast together. You being all kind and motherly and sewing buttons on my shirts. The house smelling all neat and quiet . . .
Gina	(*smiling reflectively*) I'm thinking about it too.
Kenneth	Well . . . there's going to be more to it than meets the eye, isn't there? What's going to be underneath it all?
Gina	You do want to come and live here?
Kenneth	Yes! But . . .
Gina	You are happy about it?
Kenneth	Yes, I'm *happy* . . .
Gina	*I'm* happy!
Kenneth	*I'm* happy! But . . .
Gina	But what?
Kenneth	But here we sit – we keep saying we're happy . . . What are we trying to hide from ourselves?
Gina	Are we trying to hide something from ourselves?
Kenneth	Gina, I explained it all!
Gina	But are you sure it works this way round as well?
Kenneth	Well, doesn't it? If you see somebody else leading what looks like a contented life, don't you immediately know that there are all sorts of hidden tensions and resentments underneath?

She thinks.

Gina	Perhaps what we're trying to hide from ourselves is the fact that we actually *are* happy.
Kenneth	(*doubtfully*) Yes . . . But when I think of all that happiness, stretching on and on . . .
Gina	(*cradling his head*) Oh, love, you're so young! You expect so much! What you've got to do now is to grow up just a tiny bit, and learn another of life's little lessons. You've got to understand that when you've finally got what you want in this world, you don't want what you've got after all. It's really just what you were saying yourself, isn't it? Now, I'm going to tuck you up on the couch here . . .

She does so.

And you can have a nice little snooze before lunch.

Kenneth Yes, but . . .

Gina Sh! Don't worry your head about it any more! I'm going to put the joint on. Nice crispy brown potatoes – thick squelchy Yorkshire pudding! Think of that!

She goes towards the stairs door, then turns back to him.

Just try to see it the other way round: if you don't want what you've got, that proves you've got what you want!

Kenneth (*doubtfully*) Yes . . .

Then he sees the attraction of the idea.

Yes!

And then he loses sight of it again.

Yes . . .

Fade to black.

Mr Foot

A Living Room.

Evening. **Geoffrey** *and* **Nibs** *are sitting in armchairs,
both reading solid-looking volumes. He has the air of a
don, or senior civil servant, though he is in fact neither;
she of a don's wife. For some time there is silence. Geoffrey
wrinkles his nose to slide his spectacles a little further up,
and a few seconds later she does the same. Then one of his
feet, crossed over the other knee, begins to jiggle impatiently.
It continues for some moments, with unconscious mechanical
persistence.* **Nibs** *lifts her head slightly and watches it.
He feels her eye upon him. The foot stops jiggling and he
looks up.*

Geoffrey	What?
Nibs	Foot.
Geoffrey	Ah.

*They both return to their books. After a few moments the foot
starts to jiggle again, and* **Nibs** *looks up. He immediately stops,
and uncrosses his legs. She continues to watch him, and after a
few moments he looks up from his book and returns her gaze.*

	What?
Nibs	This job . . .
Geoffrey	What job?
Nibs	This job you're in line for . . .
Geoffrey	What about it?
Nibs	You're *in line* for it?
Geoffrey	*(returning to his book)* I'm *in line* for it, yes.
Nibs	What does that mean, precisely – *in line*?
Geoffrey	*(after a pause, without looking up) In line* means *in line*. That's what *in line* means.
Nibs	Ah.

Geoffrey	(*looking up sharply*) What?
Nibs	Ah!

He returns to his book. She continues to watch him. His foot jiggles briefly.

And am *I* on show this time?

Geoffrey	(*after a pause, without looking up*) The Chairman may want to *take a squint* at you. I don't know. The firm may not be in the habit of *taking a squint* at wives. On the other hand, it may.

She stops looking at him, and gazes into space ahead of her. When she next speaks, it is directed primarily at herself.

Nibs	I suppose I shall wear the navy shantung, with a little pearl spray over the left breast . . .

She holds out her hand, smiling.

'How very kind of you to ask us . . . ! What a beautiful part of the world! What a beautiful house! What lovely girls! What handsome boys!'

She inclines her head back and to one side, with eyes closed, in a gesture of silent laughter.

'Does he? Really, the things we wives have to put up with! Do you know, up to a few years ago Geoffrey insisted on wearing his old army issue tropical shorts on the beach!'

She turns to the person sitting on the other side of her, and thrusts her chin forward challengingly.

'Now tell me the truth, Sir Harold! Isn't your company doing exactly what all those wicked Spaniards did in the seventeenth century – plundering the New World to enrich the Old? Aren't you really the conquistadors of the modern age?'

Geoffrey's *foot starts to jiggle. She smilingly offers her hand again.*

'Well, that was a wonderful evening! Thank you so much! I always adore dinner-parties, because Geoffrey's foot is hidden under the table, and I can't see whether it's on the jig or not . . .'

The foot abruptly stops jiggling.

Geoffrey (*without looking up*) Bear in mind that it may not be a dinner-party this time. They may send someone here.

She stares at him. He looks up.

It's a progressive company. They'll put a professional on the job, probably – send a *dick* round.

Nibs A *dick*? To dinner?

Geoffrey No – to watch the house. See who goes in, who comes out. See how many *boyfriends* you've got.

They both resume their reading. **Geoffrey** *smiles to himself.*

Count the *boyfriends* going in the front. Count the empties coming out the back. *Sex* and *booze* – that's the sort of thing a progressive employer wants to know about.

Nibs *looks up and watches him coldly, as he smiles to himself.*

Then no doubt he'll come to the door. Take a *dekko* at you from close to.

Nibs I shan't let him in.

Geoffrey Of course you'll let him in.

Nibs I most certainly shall not.

Geoffrey You won't know who it is. He'll be disguised as a brush salesman, or a market-research *johnny*.

Nibs I don't let brush salesmen in.

Geoffrey You'll let this one in, because these people are *professionally trained* to get into people's homes. Unless I am very much mistaken, you are not *professionally trained* to keep them out.

His foot jiggles.

Once inside, he'll no doubt start *banging off* questions.

Nibs	If he starts *banging off* questions I shall know he's not a brush salesman.
Geoffrey	Not if they're questions about brushes!
Nibs	About brushes?
Geoffrey	To begin with.
Nibs	'How often do you sweep the floor?'
Geoffrey	They will no doubt become more personal.
Nibs	'Do you clean your teeth up and down or side to side?'

His foot jiggles as he reads.

Geoffrey In any case, it won't be a brush salesman. It will be a market researcher.

They both read for some moments. Then he looks up again.

You won't have a chance to put your *fancy dress* on, you realise.

He returns to his book. She slowly lifts her head and gazes at him expressionlessly. **Geoffrey's** *foot suffers a brief spasm of jiggling, but is brought under control. She returns to her book. He looks up again.*

What will you say to him? You'd better think of something before he arrives, hadn't you? Otherwise you'll get into one of your *muddles.* I shan't be here when he comes, of course.

She slowly lifts her head.

Nibs	I shan't get into a muddle just because you're not here! It's you sitting there shaking your foot at me that gets me into my muddles.
Geoffrey	You have your muddles with or without the assistance of my foot. My foot is neither here nor there.

It jiggles briefly, and is brought under control.

	Not that it's anything to do with me, of course, whether you get into a muddle when this man calls.
Nibs	(*sarcastically*) No, if you don't get the job because I've had one of my muddles, that's nothing to do with you *at all*.
Geoffrey	I leave it entirely to you. As long as you know what you are going to say . . .
Nibs	Oh, I shall say –

To her imaginary interviewer.

	Sit down, sit down! Make yourself at home . . . !
Geoffrey	You don't have to rehearse it to me! I'm not your form-mistress!
Nibs	No, I must get it right! We don't want one of my muddles!
Geoffrey	Just run through it in your head, that's all I'm suggesting. You're not a child.
Nibs	No, no – I shall say –

To interviewer.

Do sit down! My word, you have an interesting job, going round talking to all these wives, seeing the way we live! Tell me, are we all going out of our minds with frustration and boredom, as everyone says . . . ?

To **Geoffrey**.

| | Is this right? Am I doing it right? |
| Geoffrey | It's not a question of *doing it right*. I wish you wouldn't keep asking me if you're *doing things right!* Just do what you think best! |

Geoffrey's *foot jiggles vigorously.* **Nibs** *turns back to the interviewer.*

| Nibs | Something I've always wanted to know – do any of the other wives you see have husbands with a foot problem? |

The foot stops abruptly.

Geoffrey	I'm not listening.
Nibs	(*to interviewer*) He's not listening. Nothing new in that, of course. He never does. Which is why it's rather pleasant to have someone come to the house who is actually *paid* to listen. If I say something to Geoffrey, there's always a long pause, and then . . .

A long pause. Then **Geoffrey**, *becoming at last aware that a sentence has been left hanging in the air, looks up.*

Geoffrey	(*irritably*) What?
Nibs	(*to interviewer*) It's like being sick – it's the waiting for it to happen that's the worst part. Would you like a drink?
Geoffrey	A drink? In the middle of the evening?
Nibs	(*to* **Geoffrey**) Not you. Him.
Geoffrey	Him a drink? In the middle of the day? That won't create a very good impression.
Nibs	(*to interviewer*) Whisky? Gin and something? A glass of beer perhaps?

To **Geoffrey**.

It's not even the middle of the day! It's just after breakfast, if you want to know. I haven't made the beds yet! The house is in chaos! I'm not even *dressed!*

To interviewer.

Just throw that vacuum-cleaner off the chair if it's in your way! It's like a pig-sty in here anyway . . . A gin-and-tonic? Very good idea – I'll have one too. If we really get down to it we can drink ourselves stupid before elevenses.

She mimes pouring the drinks. **Geoffrey**, *who has been watching her with distaste, returns to his book.*

Geoffrey	I'm not listening to all this rubbish, you know.
Nibs	I should hope not! Mr . . .

She looks interrogatively at her interviewer.

Samuelson, Mr Samuelson. Mr Samuelson and I are talking privately. Aren't we, Mr Samuelson? What . . . ? Oh, cheers.

She mimes raising her glass and drinking. To **Geoffrey**.

If Mr Samuelson says 'cheers' I shall say 'cheers'.

To **Mr Samuelson**.

Now, what do you want to know about me? Am I a suitable wife? Well, yes, I am, I'm an entirely suitable wife, thanks to the very thorough training that Geoffrey gave me in the early years of our marriage. 'Just be yourself,' he used to say, when we went out to dinner. 'Don't keep saying "Geoffrey says . . ." and "Geoffrey thinks . . ." Don't keep looking at me to see if I approve. Just behave naturally! But don't keep starting sentences that trail away into nothingness, and don't keep saying wild, meaningless things that end up in screams of laughter. If you can't think of anything sensible and natural to say, just smile quietly to yourself.' Of course, Geoffrey is largely retired from teaching now, but his able assistant Mr Foot carries on the good work.

Geoffrey's *foot jiggles, but is quickly brought under control.*

I lead a very full life. I read; I paint. And of course there's my *work* at the Citizen's Advice Bureau. Incidentally, I don't recall seeing you around when I applied for it, *taking a squint* at Geoffrey to see whether he was a suitable husband . . . I suppose you went round to his office, disguised as an insurance salesman . . .

To **Geoffrey**.

Did anyone come to *take a squint* at *you* when I applied for my job?

There is no reaction. She turns back reassuringly to
Samuelson.

Don't worry – we shall get a reply in two or three days at
the very outside. What can we talk about in the meantime?
You know we have two sons? Both away at university now.
Do you have to check to see if *they're* suitable . . . ?

Geoffrey (*looking up*) What?

Nibs (*to* **Samuelson**) Ah, we're through.

To **Geoffrey.**

Did anyone come to *take a squint at you* when I applied for
my job?

Geoffrey Why should anyone want to *take a squint* at me?

Nibs (*to* **Samuelson**) What I can never understand is how and
why he's managed to become so much like a Professor
of Greek, when he's in fact a successful businessman.
Let alone how he's managed to turn me into a
professor's wife.

Geoffrey's *foot jiggles.*

Geoffrey If you're trying to *take a dig* at me you're wasting your
breath. I've told you I'm not listening.

Nibs Then why is Mr Foot on the jig?

It stops.

Geoffrey I wish you wouldn't call it Mr Foot.

Nibs (*to* **Samuelson**) Mr Foot thinks I'm giving you the wrong
impression.

Geoffrey One of these days you'll start talking about Mr Foot when
there's someone around to hear.

Nibs (to **Samuelson**) We never mention Mr Foot in public,
you see.

Geoffrey You're working yourself up into one of your *muddles*. Why
don't you either get quietly on with your book, or take
some of those pills Dr Farquhar gave you and go to bed?

He returns to his book. **Nibs** *sits watching him for a moment,
apparently silenced. Then she turns discreetly back to* **Mr**

Samuelson *and, glancing cautiously at her husband to see if he is listening, gestures with the imaginary bottle to* **Mr Samuelson** *to let her recharge his glass. She pours some more for herself, conspiring with* **Mr Samuelson** *against her husband. She smiles at him and silently raises her glass to him.*

Nibs   (*in a low voice to* **Samuelson**) He doesn't like gin. He thinks it's only drunk by women, and men who join tennis clubs.

She glances at **Geoffrey** *again. Her manner suggests that the whole conversation is behind Geoffrey's back.*

He won't eat anything fried, or anything frozen, or any fruit out of a tin, or any pudding out of a packet, or anything *pretending to be Italian* . . . I sit here for hours wondering what to give him for dinner . . . I sit painting my pictures . . .

She mimes it.

. . . and what am I thinking? I'm thinking –

She speaks slowly and abstractedly, leaning forward to work on the detail of the picture.

'I wonder if *oeufs Florentine* are *pretending to be Italian?*' And then I think, 'Oh my God! He told me to ring the man about mending the fence before twelve . . . !'

She glances anxiously at her watch, then hurriedly begins to put her brushes away, and get to her feet.

'I wonder if he caught his plane to Belfast all right . . . ?'

She is just about to hurry away to the phone when another thought strikes her, and she stops, appalled.

'I did put the flask of coffee in his brief-case, didn't I? If he has to drink airline coffee there and back he'll come home this evening in a great state of silent moral outrage.

He'll sit there reading "Coins of the Greek Colonies in Italy", and Mr Foot will go jig-jig-jig-jig-jig . . .'

Mr Foot does so, but **Geoffrey** *seizes it and hold it.*

'What's the matter?' 'What? Nothing's the matter,' But Mr Foot thinks something's the matter. Disagrees with some statement in the book, perhaps. No, something I've done. I haven't wound the hall clock again . . . I've forgotten to put any stockings on . . . I've put the newspapers under the cushions . . . I've left the lavatory light on all day . . .

She sits down again, watching **Geoffrey** *apprehensively.*

'Had a good day?' – No, no, no, that's wrong! Strike that out of the record! He thinks that's suburban – something we certainly can't afford to be, living as we do in the suburbs. Let's see . . . 'How was Belfast, then?' No, no, no! I asked that about Amsterdam last week. 'How was Amsterdam?' 'What?' 'How was Amsterdam?' Jig-jig-jig-jig-jig! 'I'm afraid I didn't enquire after its health.' *Sorry*! Now . . . I know: 'Did you catch the plane all right?'

Pause.

'What?' 'Did you catch the plane all right?' 'Yes.'

Pause.

'Let's think, what can I ask him now? We can't have reached the end of our conversational resources already. 'Did you catch the plane *back* all right?'

Pause.

'What? - Yes'. All right so far! But what's this? Mr Foot's on the go! I've bored Mr Foot! Said too much! Said something vulgar! You'd never believe how easy it is to upset Mr Foot! If Mr Foot could hear what I'm telling you now he'd have to be held down!

Geoffrey *at once lets go of the foot. In an instant it starts to jiggle again. He seizes it once more. She pours* **Mr Samuelson** *and herself more drinks.*

Mr Foot would think I was representing myself as *the little woman* just to annoy him. Mr Foot doesn't like me to be *the little woman*! The medium-sized woman, yes; but not the little one . . . Cheers . . . ! Woo, I'm starting to feel rather dizzy . . . ! So let me assure you, just in case he can overhear us, just in case he's got the place bugged – oh, I wouldn't put it past him! – no, I wouldn't! – oh, he's as mad as a hatter! –

Into an imaginary microphone.

Yes, cooee, can you hear me? We're talking about you!

To **Samuelson**.

– Let me assure you I get my own back! For instance, I put frozen beans in the goulash! He never notices.

Into the microphone.

Do you hear that? Frozen beans in the goulash!

To **Samuelson**.

Though why food pretending to be Hungarian is permitted I cannot imagine . . . What else do I do? Well, I wrap the rubbish in the morning papers by mistake. I have one of my *muddles* and I forget to buy stockings, so that I have to go to the Traffords with bare legs. Yes, to the Traffords! Twice now! With absolutely nothing whatsoever around the lower legs! Just naked white skin! And when we get there, what happens? I feel another of my muddles coming on! I start every sentence with 'Geoffrey thinks . . .', 'Geoffrey says . . .', 'According to Geoffrey . . .' And I finish every sentence with '. . . don't you, Geoffrey?'

'. . . have I got that right, Geoffrey?' And Mr Foot's hidden under the table, so I never know what he thinks at all, except at the Costains, where they've got a table with wobbly legs, and I can feel the whole thing shaking with disapproval.

The imaginary table she is sitting at shakes beneath her hands. At the same moment **Geoffrey's** *foot breaks loose and jiggles. He seizes his foot. She seizes the table.*

It's this *ménage à trois* with his friend Mr Foot which is so difficult to bear.

She recharges **Mr Samuelson's** *glass and her own.*

I wonder what Foot does at the office all day. That's what I'd like to know . . . I don't know what I'm saying; I'm a little bit drunk. You'll be running away with the idea that I'm jealous of my husband's foot! It's not jealousy – it's just that I think it's getting a *hold* over him . . . which I don't think it's right for a foot to have over a man . . .

She catches sight of it, and gives a little wave and forced smile.

Hello!

To **Samuelson**.

It's watching us.

To foot, offering bottle.

Like a drink?

To **Samuelson**, *as she extends the bottle towards the foot, as if about to pour it a drink.*

I'll get it drunk. Then it might tell us a thing or two.

The foot jiggles briefly.

No?

She turns back to **Samuelson**.

It's got such a negative attitude to life, that's what I dislike so much. All it can do is disapprove! I think a healthy normal foot would try to encourage you, as well – give you a pat on the back from time to time. Don't you?

The foot jiggles briefly.

Don't take any notice of it. No, no – don't look at it. We must make plans. We'll wait till it's asleep, then overpower it. We'll put a sack over its head – tie it up – drag it to the river and throw it in. Then we'll go away. Yes, we'll run away together! We'll start a new life! We'll go to Canada – I have friends there. I'll got out to work – we won't starve . . .

Geoffrey *lifts his eyes from his book and gazes at her.*

He's listening! I told you – the whole place is bugged!

She meets his disquieted gaze. They stare at each other in silence for a moment. Then she turns back to **Samuelson.**

He heard everything! He's thinking about what to say! Whether to be outraged or understanding . . .!

She meets **Geoffrey's** *gaze again. A pause.*

Geoffrey	What's that smell? Did you leave something on the stove?
Nibs	(*to* **Samuelson**) Did I leave something on the stove!
Geoffrey	What?
Nibs	(to **Geoffrey**) No, I didn't leave anything on the stove! It's the boiler smelling again.
Geoffrey	Ah.

He returns to his book.

Nibs	Have you been listening to what I was saying?

A pause.

Geoffrey	What?
Nibs	Have you been listening?
Geoffrey	You know I never listen when you're having one of your

muddles. I just leave you to get on with it in peace and
work it out of your system.

Nibs (to **Samuelson**) He hasn't been listening. It's Foot
who listens, of course. Foot listens, and from time to
time submits reports on the situation to headquarters.
That's what all that jiggling is – it's Foot tapping out his
reports in Morse. They don't take it very seriously up
at headquarters. Old Nibs is having one of her muddles
again, they think. (Nibs is me; I'm called Nibs. Did you
know that? Unbelievable, isn't it? How did *that* happen?)
Old Nibs is holding another demonstration for women's
rights – old Nibs is marching up and down outside again
with banners and slogans. Well, that's right – it'll keep her
out of mischief; that's what Geoffrey thinks. (Here we go
again – 'Geoffrey thinks . . .' – 'Geoffrey says'!) Geoffrey
thinks I get into my muddles just to irritate him. Well,
certainly I do! Undoubtedly! But supposing one day I get
into one of my muddles and I can't get out again! They'll
cart me off to the muddlehouse! Think how Foot will
shake and dance and tap when *that* happens!

The foot suffers a spasm of jiggling

There he goes, just at the thought of it! Geoffrey will think
I've got myself in the muddlehouse just to annoy him! And
that might be true! That's what he can't stand, you see –
the thought that I don't have any existence independent of
him, that everything I do is just to please or annoy him. 'Just
be yourself!' he used to say, when he still had hopes. 'Don't
look at me all the time to see if I approve!' He wants me
to be *his*. But of course I can't be his unless I'm separate
from him – unless I remain *me*. He's like a little child with a
soap-bubble; he can't enjoy it unless he can hold it, and as
soon as he tries to hold it it vanishes. He thinks I've become
just another part of himself! And a nagging, troublesome
part at that! A tooth with the toothache! Another foot with
the shakes! And of course he feels it reflects badly on him,
having to admit to the world that he's married to his foot.
'You've met my left and right feet, but I don't think you've
met my foot Nibs, have you?'

Confidentially.

'She goes on the twitch from time to time. Don't pay any attention. It's just a slight disability I suffer from.' Well, he's going to get a surprise when he looks up from his book one day and discovers that I've run off with you to Canada! 'What? Run away with the *dick* who was sent to check that she was a suitable wife? What will the bloke put in his report now?' But he'd be even more surprised if he knew what I was thinking and talking about over there in Canada! Because it wouldn't be about him! Oh no! I shouldn't be saying, 'Geoffrey thinks . . .' and 'Geoffrey says . . .' all the time. I'd be myself! I'd be running through the forests with bare legs, living off frozen peas and tinned pears and spaghetti bolognaise out of a packet! And leaving all the lights on! And putting all the newspapers under the cushions! I'd just be laughing and laughing and laughing . . .

She laughs at the thought of it.

. . . and saying, 'how surprised Geoffrey would be, if only he could see me now . . . !'

The elation drains out of her, as she realises what she is saying.

'. . . for once not even thinking about him.'

A silence. She sits gazing in absent-minded dejection at his foot. Gradually the absence of sound makes him first jiggle the foot, then look up.

Geoffrey   What?

She doesn't respond.

All over then? Why don't you *toddle along?* Get a good night's rest in case this bloke comes?

Still no response.

Don't want to find yourself getting in one of your muddles with *him*.

Geoffrey *returns to his book.* **Nibs** *sighs, and gets up as if to go. She catches sight of his foot, and kneels down in front of it.*

Nibs   (*to the foot*) Well, then, *you* tell him. He'll listen to you. Just explain what the situation is, that's all. Just tell him – oh, I don't know – tell him . . .

The foot jiggles violently. She moves back, discouraged.

Tell him to lock up before he comes to bed.

She gets to her feet and turns to go. Curtain.

Chinamen

The dining-room of **Stephen** *and* **Jo***'s house, with the table laid for six. There are three doors leading off – one into the kitchen, one into the living-room, and the third into a corridor which gives access to lavatory, stairs, back door, etc. There is also a window overlooking the street. It is dark outside.*

Jo *enters hurriedly through the corridor door, still struggling into her dress. She begins to check the dinner table, balancing on one evening shoe and counting the cutlery with the other.*

Jo   (*at speed*) Knife knife fork fork spoon, knife knife fork fork spoon, knife knife fork fork spoon . . . Soup spoons! Oh, my God!

She hobbles hurriedly out to the kitchen, holding her unzipped dress up.

Girl Child (*off*) Mummy, can we come down and just say hello to all the people?

Jo *at once comes out of the kitchen, shouting in the direction of the corridor door.*

Jo   No! Go to sleep, both of you!

She shuts the corridor door firmly and hurries back into the kitchen. As she does so, **Stephen** *hurries in from the living-room carrying another dining-chair to add to the four around the table.*

Stephen   It's ten past eight, Jo!
Jo   Don't tell *me* it's ten past eight!

He puts the chair down and heads back at once towards the living-room.

Stephen	John and whatsit always arrive at eight-fifteen sharp for eight o'clock. Oh God, I've forgotten her name again!

He goes out into the living-room. **Jo** *re-emerges from the kitchen, carrying soup spoons.*

Jo	*Laura!* John and Laura! It's getting the children to bed that does it – we'll *have* to get another *au pair*, Stephen . . . Oh, not that one . . . that's the one with the dicky leg.

She picks up the chair which **Stephen** *has just brought in, and hurries it out to the kitchen, still holding spoons, shoe, and dress. As she does so,* **Stephen** *hurries back in from the living-room carrying another chair.*

Stephen	Laura, Laura, Laura . . . My block about names gets worse and worse every day!
Jo	Get another chair out of the living-room, Stephen. I'm putting the dicky one in the kitchen so no one can sit on it by mistake.

She goes out.

Stephen	(*putting down the chair he is carrying, and heading back for another*) David and *Laura!* David and *Laura!* David and *Laura* . . . !

He goes out into the living-room as **Jo** *returns from the kitchen.*

Jo	*John* and Laura! *John* and Laura. For heaven's sake get it straight, Stephen. We've known them for ten years!

She starts hurriedly distributing soup spoons, as **Stephen** *hurries back in with another chair.*

Stephen	I can't really tell our friends apart, that's the trouble. John and Laura, John and Laura, John and Laura . . . They're exactly the same – same age, same number of children, same sort of job, same income, same opinions . . .
Jo	(*surveying the table*) Zip me up, will you?

Stephen	(zipping her) They even look alike! It's like looking at Chinamen. Nicholas and Jay – Simon and Kay – Freddie and Di . . .
Jo	No doubt they think the same about us. Have you put the ice out for the drinks?
Stephen	Yes . . . Good God, *we're* not like that! Are we?
Jo	Now, John can sit at the head of the table . . .
Stephen	John and Laura, John and Laura, John and Laura . . .
Jo	Then Laura can sit *here* . . .
Stephen	(*indicating*) Bee next to John. John and Laura, John and Laura . . . Barney over there. At least I won't forget *their* names! Barney and Bee, my God!
Jo	(*gazing at him, appalled*) Not Barney and Bee, Stephen!
Stephen	What do you mean, not Barney and Bee? Of course it's Barney and Bee
Jo	Stephen!
Stephen	Barney and Bee! Barney and Bee! I might forget David and Dora, but *Barney and Bee* .. !
Jo	Stephen, she's left him! Bee's left Barney!
Stephen	No!
Jo	I *told* you!
Stephen	I don't remember that.
Jo	She couldn't stand it any longer! She just quietly left, without any fuss, about a week ago, and went off with a man called Alex!
Stephen	(*rubbing his chin and struggling to focus his mind*) Oh . . . Some faint memory does stir. A singer, or something, wasn't he?
Jo	He runs one of those psychedelic discotheque places.
Stephen	So it's not Barney and Bee any more?
Jo	No, darling. Alex and Bee.
Stephen	Alex and Bee. It doesn't sound very convincing somehow, does it?
Jo	Well, that's what it is. You won't forget again, will you, Stephen?
Stephen	Alex and Bee . . . Alex and Bee . . . Thank God you told me! So Barney'll be coming on his own tonight?
Jo	No, no, no – it's not Barney who's coming! It's Bee, and she's bringing Alex, so that we can meet him. Oh God – no napkins!

She runs out to the kitchen to fetch them. He stands gazing after her, the ramifications of the situation slowly dawning on him.

Stephen   (*appalled*) Alex and Bee are coming here tonight?

Jo   (*running back in with the napkins*) Yes, *Alex and Bee.* Do get it straight, darling.

She rapidly distributes the napkins as **Stephen** *gazes at her.*

Well, at least Alex will make a change from all the Chinamen. According to Sara Dolomore he's about nineteen, with hair down to his shoulders, and strings of beads, and dingle-dangles all over him . . . What are you looking like that for, Stephen?

Stephen   Jo, I've done a terrible thing!

Jo   What do you mean?

Stephen   Well, I ran into Barney at lunchtime today. I'd entirely forgotten about Bee leaving him . . .

Jo   (*despairingly*) So you asked after her? You said, 'And how is your very lovely wife?'

Stephen   No. I said, 'See you this evening, then.'

Jo   Stephen, you didn't!

Stephen   And he said, 'This evening? What do you mean?' And I said, 'You're coming to dinner this evening!'

Jo   And he said, 'No, I'm not – you must have mixed me up with Simon, or Mark, or Nicholas.' I bet you felt a fool!

Stephen   No, he said, 'Thanks, Stephen. You don't know how much that means to me just at the moment.' I thought at the time it was a slightly odd thing to say.

Jo   Oh, my God!

Stephen   Anyway, so I said, 'Eight o'clock, then!' And he said, 'Eight o'clock!'

They both look at their watches, and then stare at each other.

Jo   (*wildly*) Well, ring him up! Stop him!

Stephen   It's no good ringing him at a quarter past eight! He'll be on his way – he's probably on the doorstep now!

Jo   What a bloody stupid thing to do!

Stephen	Bloody stupid thing inviting your lot, if it comes to that! Fancy inviting Bee without Barney and not telling me!
Jo	I did tell you! You just weren't listening, you stupid oaf!
Stephen	Well, fancy not making sure I was listening! Anyway, I *was* listening. I wasn't remembering, that's all.
Jo	You weren't remembering!
Stephen	Oh, for heaven's sake don't waste time arguing!
Jo	I'm not the one who's wasting time . . . !
Stephen	(*shouting*) All right, then! So let's decide what we're going to do before . . .

The front door bell rings. They gaze at each other.

Jo	Don't let them in!
Stephen	We've got to let them in! Anyway, that'll be David and whatsit, David and Nora.
Jo	John and Laura.

As she speaks she goes to the window and tries to see them through the crack in the curtains.

	But we musn't let *anyone* in till we've thought out what we're going to do.
Stephen	Oh, for heaven's sake! They'll all be meeting on the doorstep!
Jo	Well, at least if they meet on the doorstep we shan't have to watch.
Stephen	Perhaps the first thing is to decide exactly what we're trying to do. Why are we so frightened of them meeting? Are we trying to spare their feelings, or is it just our own embarrassment that we're worried about?
Jo	I've a good mind to walk out the back door and leave you to get on with it.
Stephen	My God! If anyone should be walking out it's me! I mean, let's reason this out one step at a time . . .

The bell rings again. They stare at each other, undecided. Then **Stephen** *gives in.*

Oh . . . !

He hurries out through the living-room. **Jo** *rushes to the window for another look through the crack in the curtains, then runs to the mirror and has a last quick look at herself. Then she goes to the living-room door and opens it a crack, listening to hear who it is.*

Stephen   (*jovially, off*) . . . No, no, no, not late at all. Just right. Come in and sit yourselves down . . .

She shuts the door, hurries to the table, and distractedly dabs at the cutlery. **Stephen** *reappears from the living room, still speaking to* **John** *and* **Laura** *as he turns to shut the door.*

Excuse me a moment. One or two little . . . you know . . .

He nods jovially to complete the sense, then shuts the door and turns tensely to face **Jo.**

David and Dora . . .
Jo   John and Laura.
Stephen   What are we going to do?

He opens the door again and calls jovially off to **John** *and* **Laura.**

Fix yourselves drinks, will you, um . . . ?
Jo   John.
Stephen   John.

He shuts the door and turns back to **Jo.**

We must have a clear and definite plan of campaign.

He opens the door and continues jovially to **John** *and* **Laura.**

Over there! On the side! Right . . .

He shuts the door and turns back to **Jo.**

We can't just stand here and wait for it to happen.

Jo	No, well, look . . .

She beckons him urgently over to the window to show him what she has in mind.

	You go down and wait outside the front door, and when Barney arrives, get rid of him.
Stephen	Get rid of him? How?
Jo	I don't know. Make something up. Tell him the children are infectious – tell him the pipes have burst. Tell him the truth, why not? We've known him for long enough. He'll see the funny side of it.
Stephen	'Barney, a rather amusing mistake has occurred! We didn't really mean to invite *you* at all – it was your wife and her new boyfriend we meant . . . !'
Jo	(*bundling him towards the living-room door*) Tell him something else, then.
Stephen	He's going to be terribly hurt whatever I tell him. He was setting so much store by this.
Jo	If the worst comes to the worst, take him out to a restaurant, and I'll tell the others you've been called away on business . . .

Still extremely reluctant, he allows himself to be bundled through the living-room door. As it opens they both compose their faces for their guests.

Stephen	(*jovially to* **John** *and* **Laura**) Got drinks then? Good, good, good. Sit down and relax – I'm just passing through . . .

He disappears.

Jo	Hello! Hello! No, don't get up! I'm just putting my head round the door! I've got one or two . . . you know . . .

She gestures vaguely behind her.

In the kitchen . . . and the children . . . terrible muddle . . . completely disorganised, I'm afraid . . . ! Anyway, I'm glad you managed to get here all right . . .

She smiles reassuringly, and shuts the door. Then she runs to the window, draws the curtains back, and looks out. She opens the window, calls to **Stephen** *in a stage whisper, enunciating carefully.*

Stephen! If Alex and Bee arrive first, I'll let them in. *You* hide behind the dustbins, and wait for Barney.

She draws the curtains again and goes back to the living-room to address a few more words to her guests.

All right still? Good. You will keep helping yourselves to drinks, won't you? Oh, that reminds me . . .

She shuts the living-room door and hurries back to the window. She draws the curtains back and calls to **Stephen**.

Have you got any money on you, if you have to take Barney out . . . ? *Money* . . . ! Hold on, then . . .

She hurries back to the living-room and opens the door.

How are you both these days? I don't think I ever asked you . . .

She makes a brief foray into the living-room as she says this, and continues without pause as she emerges holding her handbag.

Do pour yourselves another drink – I've got to pay the milkman . . .

She shuts the door and returns to the window, where she throws the money out to **Stephen**.

Here you are. Five pounds, all I've got . . .

The corridor door opens, and **Barney** *looks in.* **Jo** *is still leaning out of the window.*

> But don't take him if you can possibly get shot of him by
> any other . . .

Barney (*tapping with belated discretion on the door*) Anyone at home?

Jo spins guiltily around, drawing the curtains behind her.

Jo Barney!

Barney I came the back way, I hope you don't mind. There's some
rather thuggish-looking customer lurking about on your
front doorstep. Drug-addict, probably, looking for money.

He kisses her.

Jo (*confused*) Barney, I was just going to . . . We were just
thinking . . .

Barney I hope I'm not late.

He hands her his briefcase and umbrella.

> Been sitting in the pub ever since six o'clock. Couldn't
> face going home to an empty house. Just waiting for the
> moment to come round here. Then when the time came
> . . . I thought I'd have another drink first. You know
> how it is, when you're just killing time.

Jo Barney, there's something I've got to tell you right away,
before you come in . . .

Barney Thanks, Jo – but let's not even talk about it. I know how
you feel.

Jo I'm terribly sorry about Bee, Barney. I really am. Look, I
don't quite know how to put this, but . . .

Barney I know – you just don't know what to say to someone
when something like this happens, do you? I don't know
what to say about it myself. Ten years, and then – woof!
It's quite a shock.

Jo Yes. But the thing is, Barney . . .

Barney She's gone off with someone in ear-rings – hair
halfway down his back. I mean how does that make
me look? It makes me a complete laughing-stock,
doesn't it?

Jo Yes, but listen, Barney . . .

Barney I haven't so far had the pleasure of making his

acquaintance. I'm about the only person in town who hasn't, I may say. Do you know what she's done? She's wheeled him round to meet all our old friends, to get them all on her side! Wherever I go I find people have just had them to dinner! Then when I turn up they're embarrassed. They don't want to know me. People who have been friends for years!

Jo   Barney . . .

Barney   I mean, I take it you haven't just . . .

Jo   No, no, no. But . . .

Barney   It's always the same when a couple splits up. No one wants to take sides, but everyone does.

Jo   Yes, but . . .

Barney   I was just going to say, that's why I'm so very touched to be invited here tonight . . . Sorry, you were going to say something.

She looks at him as if she is, then changes her mind.

Jo   No, no. Just that . . . it's very nice to see you.

Barney   (*putting his arm round her, and leading her towards the living-room*) Bless you, Jo. You really find out who your friends are when something like this happens. Where's Stephen? In here?

Jo   (*stopping short*) Oh, my God, I'd forgotten all about him! He's just . . . fixing something outside. I'd better give him a call.

She leads **Barney** *firmly towards the kitchen.*

Now why don't you sit down quietly in the kitchen for a moment? Then we can have a little chat about things together while I'm getting the dinner.

Barney   (*turning at the kitchen door*) Jo, you're a real brick. You and Stephen – don't you ever . . .

Jo   Oh, no.

Stephen   I mean, old Stephen's like me. He may not seem very exciting, and so on, but . . .

Jo   Don't worry, Barney.

Barney   You're still . . . ?

He links his little fingers together and pulls, in a gesture indicating solid attachment.

Jo   Yes.
Barney   (*patting her on the shoulder*) Good girl.

She at last manages to get the door shut on him, and at once hurries across to the window. Just as she is drawing the curtains back, **Barney** *puts his head out from the kitchen again.*

Barney   (*wagging his finger*) I'm serious about that, Jo.
Jo   (*whirling round to face* **Barney**) Yes. Stay there, Barney. I'll bring you a drink.

He goes back into the kitchen, leaving the door open. **Jo** *opens the curtains with great precaution, and, glancing anxiously over her shoulder at the open kitchen door, mouths silently to* **Stephen**.

Barney's here! Come back!

She pantomines desperately, pointing at the kitchen and indicating that he should return. At last, evidently satisfied that he has understood, she closes the curtains and goes to the kitchen.

What would you like – whisky?

She hurries to the living-room, addressing **John** *and* **Laura** *as she dives briefly in and emerges again holding up a bottle of whisky.*

How's Midge enjoying school . . . ? Need a drop of whisky for the soup – there's another bottle on the side. Do keep helping yourselves.

She shuts the living-room door and hurries to the kitchen, where she hands the bottle through the open door to an arm which emerges to take it.

Fix it yourself, will you, Barney? There's ice in the fridge . . .

*Having taken the bottle, the arm takes her hand, drawing it off, evidently to **Barney's** lips. There is the sound of a kiss.*

Oh, Barney!

She flutters her eyelashes, in hurried appreciation.

Anyway, make yourself at home. I've just got to . . . you know . . . this and that . . .

*She shuts the kitchen door. As she does so, the living-room door opens and **Stephen** enters, talking jovially to **John** and **Laura**.*

Stephen   That's right! Ships that pass in the night! Anyway, pour yourselves another drink . . .

*He closes the door and turns to face **Jo**.*

    What is it?
Jo   He's here! Barney! He came in round the back.
Stephen   Oh, my God!
Jo   I've put him in the kitchen.
Stephen   In the kitchen?
Jo   In case Alex and Bee arrived before I could warn you.
Stephen   (*irritated*) You should have got rid of him.

He goes to the kitchen, turning instantly jovial as he opens the door.

Stephen   Hello! Barney! Nice to see you!
Barney   (*off*) Stephen!
Stephen   (*emerging again, still holding **Barney's** hand*) Don't get up! Stay where you are! Got something to keep you occupied, have you? Anyway, pour yourself a drink. Oh, you have. That's the spirit!

*He smilingly disengages himself, shuts the door, and turns furiously upon **Jo**.*

Why didn't you get rid of him?

Jo	Oh, Stephen, I couldn't! He kept thanking me for inviting him – he thinks we're the only friends he's got left. He made me feel such a heel for inviting Alex and Bee.
Stephen	Oh, for God's sake! We can't start being sentimental at this stage!
Jo	(*with asperity*) Well, *you* get rid of him!
Stephen	I can't get rid of him *now!* Now you've set him up in the kitchen with a bottle of Scotch!
Jo	Well, we'll just have to get rid of Alex and Bee instead.
Stephen	How?
Jo	I suppose you'll have to go down and wait outside the front door again.

Stephen *compresses his lips with reluctance.*

Stephen	Supposing they come round the back, like Barney?
Jo	(*pushing him towards the living-room door*) Keep an eye on the back as well! Patrol back and forth! Good heavens, you were in the army – you know how to guard things.

But just as he is about to open the living-room door, he rebels.

Stephen	Look, I can't just walk straight past David and Nora again!
Jo	John and Laura. Well, go out the back way, then!

Jo *urges* **Stephen** *towards the corridor door.*

Just get out there fast, that's all that matters, because any moment now they're going to be ringing that . . .

The front door bell rings. **Stephen** *and* **Jo**, *already holding the corridor door open, freeze. They gaze at each other in silence for a moment.*

Stephen	*Now* what are we going to do?
Jo	Well, we'll just have to . . . I don't know . . . shout at them out of the window.
Stephen	Shout at them out of the window?
Jo	Explain what the situation is. Tell them to go away.
Stephen	Go on, then.

Jo *crosses to the window, and looks out through the crack in the curtain, irresolute. She makes as if to shout, but gives up.*

Jo	Or we could just pretend not to be here. How about that?

The bell rings again. As they stand undecided, the kitchen door begins to open. They notice it at once.

	Barney!
Stephen	(*hurrying to bundle* **Barney** *back into the kitchen*) Sit down, Barney! Have another drink!

He goes into the kitchen, while **Jo** *hovers anxiously at the door.*

Barney	(*off*) I just thought you might like me to answer the bell, Stephen.
Jo	No, no, no, no!
Stephen	(*re-emerging*) No, no, no, no!
Jo	Just sit down and relax!
Stephen	We'll be out there to chat in a minute.

They close the kitchen door, and look at each other. The front door bell rings again.

Jo	You'll *have* to answer it. Just open the door and send them away.

She urges him towards the living-room.

	Just open the door, and explain everything quietly to them in the hall. They're reasonable people – they'll understand. Well, Bee's a reasonable person. She'll understand.
Stephen	(*hesitating, his hand on the door handle*) Bee? She's one of the least reasonable people I've ever come across.
Jo	Well, whatever you tell them, do it quickly, before they've got their coats off.

With the utmost reluctance **Stephen** *opens the door, switching on his jovial manner as he does so.*

Stephen	Here I am again then!

His face falls.

Bee!

He turns to exchange one brief horror-stricken glance with **Jo**.

They're in!

He at once turns back towards his guests, reassembling his face even as his head turns.

Bee, how lovely to see you! And this must be Alex!

Stephen *advances into the living-room.* **Jo** *closes the door behind him, in a state of shock.*

Jo Oh, my *Gawd!*

At once the living-room door reopens and **Stephen** *emerges, smiling jovially back at* **Alex** *and* **Bee**.

Stephen Well, sit down! Make yourselves at home!

He shuts the door, and turns haggardly to **Jo**.

	Dick and Dora let them in!
Jo	John and Laura!
Stephen	They've got their coats off! They're sitting down making themselves at home already!

He opens the door and calls jovially into the room.

	Pour them drinks, will you, um . . . ?
Jo	John.
Stephen	John.

He shuts the door.

You were quite right about that Alex man. I've never seen anything like it – I can't imagine what Bee was thinking of. Well, what are we going to do? We can't go and chuck them out now they're sitting down with drinks in their hands talking to Thingummy and Whatsit, can we?

Jo	No. Well I suppose they'll all three of them just have to be very adult and mature about it and face facts.
Stephen	You mean, face each other?
Jo	Well, there's nothing else for it, is there?
Stephen	This Alex lad doesn't look very adult or mature to me. I don't think his voice has broken yet.
Jo	Well, Barney and Bee will just have to be adult and mature about it.
Stephen	Bee's got her funny tense look on. At the slightest provocation she's going to burst into tears, or start playing Truth or Dare.
Jo	We'll have to tell them Barney's here, Stephen. There's no way out of it.
Stephen	Well, I refuse. Point blank.
Jo	I'll do it then.
Stephen	All right.

__Jo__ goes to the door and stands for a moment, thinking what she is going to say, trying out various social faces. Then she turns briefly back to **Stephen**, *who is watching her anxiously.*

Jo	You go and prepare Barney.

Then she turns back to the door, puts on her social face, and at once throws the door open.

Bee! How lovely to see you! *Super* dress . . . !

She advances into the room, closing the door behind her.
Stephen *grimaces after her, then reluctantly addresses himself to the job in the kitchen. He hesitates outside the kitchen door, thinking how he's going to broach the subject, then flings it open with determination and a jovial smile.*

Stephen	How are you doing out here? Plenty to drink? Good . . . Er . . .

He holds a sustained middle 'er', as if trying to remember what he is going to do next. Then, as if he has remembered and discovered that it lies elsewhere, he concludes the 'er' with a brisk 'ah' and shuts the door. He has another think, drumming his fingertips on his front teeth, then resolutely flings open the door again. He repeats the sustained 'er', exactly as before, then notices **Barney***'s briefcase and umbrella. He hands them into the kitchen, as if this has been his intention all the time.*

Your stuff!

He shuts the door. As he does so, the living-room door opens and **Jo** *comes out, laughing, and still talking to the occupants of the room.*

Jo	. . . Of course not! I've been wanting to meet Alex for – oh, a week now! Pour yourselves another drink . . .

She closes the door and turns to face **Stephen***.*

Stephen	Well, what did they say?
Jo	(*gloomily*) I didn't tell them. What did Barney say?
Stephen	I didn't tell him.
Jo	It would have been one thing if Barney had just happened to be in the room when they'd come in. But you can't just say brightly in the middle of the conversation, 'Oh, by the way, we've got your husband out in the kitchen!'
Stephen	That was where it all went wrong, putting Barney in the kitchen.
Jo	It just doesn't seem natural. It's either got to happen naturally or not at all.
Stephen	It was your fault, putting him in the kitchen. I can't think what you were up to.
Jo	It seemed perfectly logical at the time.
Stephen	Anyway . . .
Jo	Anyway, we'll just have to find a way of doing it. We'll have to feed them separately, that's what it comes down to. We'll serve all this lot dinner in the living-room, and we'll give Barney his dinner in the kitchen. I think that's the answer, isn't it?

She hurries to the dinner-table, and sets to work to off-load one complete place setting on to a tray.

Stephen	But just a moment. Where will *we* have dinner – you and I? With Barney, or with the other lot?
Jo	Well . . . . we'll rush back and forth between the two.
Stephen	They'll think that's a bit odd, won't they?
Jo	I don't see why. The host and hostess are always rushing in and out at dinner-parties. I'll run backwards and forwards with the food. You run backwards and forwards with the wine.

Jo *hands* **Stephen** *the loaded tray.*

There, that's for Barney. We'll be one short in there, but I don't suppose I'll have time to sit down, anyway. Now, just give me a hand with this table . . .

He puts the tray aside, and helps her carry the table to the living-room door.

Oh, come on! Don't look so doom-laden about it! We've had awkward situations at dinner-parties before, haven't we? If you give a dinner-party you expect something like this to happen! We'll cope! It's always been all right before!

Stephen	I sometimes wonder if life is worth living.

He opens the door and backs into the living-room, addressing the occupants jovially.

Here we are then! Meals on wheels!

He disappears from view. The table is edged slowly through the door.

Jo	I thought it would make a change to eat out here for once! It gets such a bore, always using the dining-room for dining, and the living-room for living . . .

Further progress is halted by some obstacle off, so that **Jo** *remains on stage holding her end of the table, edging it up and down and back and forth as she speaks.*

Mind the lamp, darling! John, would you move that china albatross thing before Stephen . . .

There is a crash of breaking china.

Never mind! I always hated it! Just kick the bits under the sofa . . . Darling, we can't stand here all night . . . ! Well, lift your end *over* John's head . . .

The offstage end of the table goes up, so that everything on it begins to slide towards **Jo.** *She desperately raises her end.*

Down! Your end down!

The offstage end goes down, so that everything slides the other way. She lowers her end.

Sorry, John! Was that your head under there?

Barney   (*emerging from the kitchen, holding his glass of whisky*) Jo, is there anything I can do?

Jo *desperately shoves the table out and slams the door on it.*

Jo   No, thanks Barney! Just getting the place straight. You go back and make yourself comfortable in the kitchen.

She tries to urge him along, but he stands his ground. He is now quite noticeably drunk.

Barney   It's awfully lonely in the kitchen, Jo. I've got no one to talk to out there.

Jo   I'll be out there in a moment. Have another drink.

Barney   I've had another drink. I've had several drinks. Ah, Jo!

He looks round the room sentimentally.

This room brings back memories! All the times Bee and I have been here, all the happy times we had together . . . This used to be the dining-room. You used to have a dining-table in here. . .

He crosses to where the dining-chairs still stand, marking the

*spot from which the table went. He sits down on one of the
chairs, as if he were at the table, while **Jo** shoots anxious glances
in the direction of the living room.*

You and Stephen . . . Bee and Me . . . Simon and Kay
. . . Nicholas and Jay . . . the glasses gleaming in the
candle-light . . . We used to talk about our children, do
you remember? The little tricks they'd been up to – the
funny things they'd said. And where we'd been on holiday,
and what John and Laura were doing these days. Now it's
all over. Even the table's gone.

Jo *hands him the tray with the single place setting on it.*

Jo	There's a perfectly good table in the kitchen, Barney. Now you take this along with you, and I'll be out there to give you some soup in half a tick.
Barney	(*taking the tray, and looking at it suspiciously*) I'm not going to be eating all on my own, am I?
Jo	No, no, no. That's just to be starting with. I'll bring the rest of the stuff in a minute.
Barney	(*holding the tray with one hand and putting the other arm round* **Jo**) Don't you leave me, Jo. You're the only friend I've got left in the whole wide world. Well, there's Stephen. Where is Stephen? Why's he never around when anyone wants him? Every time I come in, he goes out! I don't think Stephen likes me.
Jo	Of course he likes you, Barney. Now, come on, this way . . .
Barney	I probably shouldn't say this, Jo, but you're wasted on Stephen. Do you know that? I've always thought so. Time after time I've sat at that table . . .

*He attempts to return to the site of the table, but she restrains
him.*

	. . . and thought, My God, fancy a marvellous girl like Jo being married to a man like Stephen!
Jo	Now, come on, Barney . . .
Barney	I mean, old Stephen . . . well, he's a bit of a stick, isn't he?

Not really your type, I should have thought. Not *my* type, I can tell you that.

Jo	I thought you thought he was just like you?
Barney	Do you really think so? If I'd been around at the right time you wouldn't have thought that! Old Stephen wouldn't have stood a chance. I've always been secretly in love with you, Jo. It's not just something I'm saying because Bee's left me . . . Left me for someone in ear-rings, did you know that?
Jo	Yes. In here, Barney . . .
Barney	(*suspiciously*) How do you know that?
Jo	You told me.
Barney	Just walked out without a word. Last Wednesday evening. Hair down to here, by all accounts. Well, I ask you, what sort of position does that leave *me* in . . . ?

She at last manages to push him into the kitchen.

Jo	Now you just sit down and relax, and . . . well . . . pour yourself another drink.

She shuts the door firmly, hurries across to the dining-chairs, and takes the first two to the living-room door. She is just about to open the door when the kitchen door bursts open again, and **Barney** *comes out.*

Barney	(*shouting furiously*) But if I ever get my hands on him I'll shake him till his ear-rings drop off!
Jo	(*hurrying to put him away again*) Sh! You'll wake the children!
Barney	(*contritely*) Oh, the children . . . yes . . . Sorry, Jo. Sorry.

She pushes him back towards the kitchen.

Let me give you a kiss to show I'm forgiven . . .

Barney *kisses* **Jo** *clumsily as she bundles him away. She shuts the door, then returns to the chairs. She brings the remaining four down to the living-room door. The kitchen door opens again.* **Jo** *turns upon it, raises her finger sternly and says 'uh!', as if to make a dog sit down. The door closes again. She opens the living-room door and begins to move the chairs inside.*

Jo	(*merrily*) Chairs! I knew I'd forgotten something . . . ! You're all very quiet in here! Stephen, are you making sure everybody's got plenty to drink?

As she hands in the last chair, **Stephen** *emerges, calling back jovially over his shoulder.*

Stephen	David, pour everyone another drink, will you? And do sit down! Bee, you be mother and arrange everyone . . .

He closes the door, and turns anxiously to **Jo**.

	What's going on? Where have you been? They're all just getting silently plastered in there, waiting for something to happen.
Jo	I've been dealing with Barney. He's just getting noisily plastered in *there*. Thinks he ought to have married me.
Stephen	David and Laura shut up like clams at the sight of Alex. Alex hasn't said anything yet, and Bee just keeps looking at him anxiously, as if he might disappear in front of her eyes. For God's sake let's start to eat, before something happens.
Jo	I'll get the soup, you get the wine.

She goes out to the kitchen, he to the living-room.

Stephen	(*jovially, as he enters*) All right?
Jo	(*likewise*) All right?
Stephen	That's right . . .
Jo	All right . . .

They both reappear immediately, he with a bottle of wine which was previously on the table, she with a tureen of soup.

Stephen	(*to the occupants of the living-room, as he leaves*) Just got to put some wine in the soup.
Jo	(*to* **Barney** *as she leaves the kitchen*) Just got to put some soup in the *au pair* . . .

They cross at speed.

Stephen	(*furiously*) But why does it always happen to *us?*
Jo	Stephen, it's going to be all right!

Stephen *goes into the kitchen, she into the living-room.*

Stephen	(*to* **Barney**, *as he enters*) Wine that maketh glad the heart of man . . . !
Jo	(*to the occupants of the living-room, as she enters*) Soup! Soup! Beautiful soup!

They reappear almost at once, **Stephen** *still holding the bottle of wine,* **Jo** *now holding a single bowl of soup.*

Stephen	(*to* **Barney**, *as he leaves the kitchen*) Don't worry – I'll be back. Just got to give the *au pair* a drop.
Jo	(*to the occupants of the living-room, as she leaves*) Yes, I'll be sitting down in a moment. Just got to drop this in on the *au pair*.

They cross at speed again.

Stephen	By God, you're right! He's as pissed as a newt!
Jo	Some of them are pretty glassy-eyed in there.

Jo *goes into the kitchen,* **Stephen** *into the living room.*

Stephen	(*to the occupants of the living-room as he enters*) Wine that maketh glad the heart of man!
Jo	(*to* **Barney**, *as she enters the kitchen*) Soup of the evening! Beautiful soup!

They reappear at once, **Jo** *empty-handed,* **Stephen** *carrying the bread-basket.*

Stephen	(*to the occupants of the living-room, as he leaves*) No peace for the wicked!
Jo	(*to* **Barney**, *as she leaves the kitchen*) A woman's work is never done!

They cross at speed.

Stephen	(*desperately*) They're not saying anything!

Jo	Say something yourself then! Make conversation!

Jo goes into the living-room, **Stephen** *into the kitchen.*

Stephen	(*to* **Barney,** *as he enters*) You know where Simon and Kay say Nicholas and Jay are going this year . . . ?
Jo	(*to the occupants of the living-room, as she enters*) Have you heard that story of Nicholas and Jay's about Marcus and Poo . . . ?

They re-emerge almost at once, **Stephen** *still carrying the bottle of wine,* **Jo** *empty-handed.*

Stephen	(*to* **Barney,** *as he leaves*) . . . and was last seen walking stark naked down Kensington High Street carrying a garden sprinkler and a double bass!
Jo	(*to the occupants of the living-room, as she leaves*) . . . to which she replied, 'But Mummy, if you put some toys in your tummy too, then he won't *need* to come out'!

They close their respective doors and lean wearily against them as they catch each other's eyes.

Stephen	Not a flicker.
Jo	Heavens, we've got a slow house in here tonight!
Stephen	It's playing these audiences of one out in the sticks that depresses me. How many more courses?
Jo	Only three.

She indicates the living-room.

You go and sit down in there and talk to them while they have their soup. I'll just get the next course out of the oven, then I'll join you.

Stephen *crosses wearily to the living-room. She kisses him in passing.*

Pour yourself a drink. Just relax and enjoy yourself!

He gives her a hopeless look. She opens the door for him, and without breaking step he is transformed into the jovial host again.

Stephen (*to the occupants of the living-room*) Did I ever tell you that story of Nicholas and Kay's about Simon and Sue . . . ?

Jo *shuts the door behind him and crosses to the kitchen.*

Jo (*to* **Barney**, *as she enters*) Shall I tell you where Simon and Kay say Nicholas and Jay are going this year . . . ?

She backs out hurriedly.

No, Barney! Now just sit down like a good boy and eat up your soup. I haven't come out here for fun and games. I've just come to fetch the casserole.

She goes in again and emerges hurriedly once more, now holding a hot and heavy casserole dish away from her, looking as if she is trying to avoid having her bottom pinched. She turns to face him, and addresses him as if he were one of her children.

No, Barney! No, it's no good looking at me like that, either. I'm not amused.

She sets down the casserole so that she can close the door.

Now just you stay here and eat up all your soup and don't come out until I tell you.

She shuts the door, picks up her casserole, and takes it across to the living-room. She is just opening the door when she realises the kitchen door has opened again. She closes the living-room door with weary patience.

Now, Barney, what is it? I thought I told you to stay there and finish your dinner.

Barney (*emerging, and raising his hand*) Please, Miss, can I be excused?

Jo (*sighing impatiently*) Well, I suppose if you must, you must.

She nods at the corridor door.

Through there, turn left, second door on the right.

Barney Thank you, Miss.

He turns towards the corridor door.

Jo   But straight back to the kitchen when you've finished!

She takes the casserole into the living-room, trying simultaneously to smile at the occupants and to make sternly sure that **Barney** *is not looking in. As soon as the door shuts* **Barney** *stops, in fuddled indignation.*

Barney   Turn left, second on the right! I've been here once or twice before, you know! I'm an old friend of yours – remember? It's the same story everywhere. They all say how sorry they are, and then they don't want to know you. But this is a new one, I must say, inviting you round and then leaving you to eat on your own in the kitchen, without even the *au pair* girl for company . . . ! It's not catching, you know! My God, when I think of all the dinner-parties Bee and I gave for *them!* All the ghastly evenings I've spent *here*, sitting at the table in this very room . . . !

He goes towards where it was, shaking his head.

Now even the table has gone.

He stops in his tracks, his lachrymose mood dispelled by astonishment.

Now even the *chairs* have gone!

He gazes round in bewilderment.

What's happening here? They must have . . . They must have taken them out for spring cleaning. Or perhaps . . . they took them out and *sold* them! Well, poor bloody old Stephen and Jo! On their uppers, and never said a word about it! Gave me a bowl of soup when they can't even afford to eat themselves! What a couple of real bricks they are! I must say, you really find out who your friends are when this kind of thing happens. Jo! Stephen! Where are you?

He goes towards the living-room door.

There's no need to hide yourselves away! I know what's going on!

He stops, with his hand on the door handle, as another thought strikes him.

Oh, I was just going to have a pee, wasn't I . . .

Barney *crosses to the corridor, turning as he goes out to call reassuringly back towards the living-room.*

Don't worry – I'll be right back! What a couple of bricks!

He goes out. As he does so, the living-room door opens, and **Alex** *enters. He is a beardless young man with a great mop of frizzy hair and bell-bottomed trousers, and is hung about with chains and dingle-dangles; almost completely ambiguous as to sex and class.* **Jo's** *hand shoots out of the living-room door, catches him, and pulls him back.*

Jo	(*off*) Alex! Where are you going?
Alex	(*reappearing*) I'm just looking for, you know, the gents.

He shuts the door and crosses to the corridor door. Not seeing what he wants out there, he tries the kitchen door. He is just about to open it when the living-room door is flung open, and **Stephen** *rushes out, still clasping the bottle of wine.*

Stephen (*urgently*) *Alex*! No!

Alex *abandons the kitchen door as if it had been suddenly electrified, and starts back.* **Stephen** *hurriedly closes the living-room door and runs across to interpose himself bodily between* **Alex** *and the kitchen door.*

	Not in there, Alex!
Alex	Oh, sorry. I was just looking for, you know, the kind of, you know . . .
Stephen	Well, you won't find it in there!

Alex	(*staring at the door curiously in spite of himself*) Oh, sorry.
Stephen	This is the kitchen.
Alex	Sorry.
Stephen	(*steering him towards the corridor door*) No, no, no – my fault. I should have shown you where it was in the first place.
Alex	Well, you know, I didn't want to sort of, you know, put you sort of *out*, like.
Stephen	No, no, no – very remiss of me.

He opens the corridor door.

It's just that you looked so much at home here that I'd forgotten you hadn't been to the house before.

Alex	Oh, well, you know . . .
Stephen	But I hope we'll be seeing a lot of you and Bee in the future. In a few months time you'll be able to find the way to the john here in your sleep.
Alex	(*as he is gradually edged through the door*) Oh, well . . . Yeah, that'd be nice . . .
Stephen	Turn left, second on the right.

He closes the door, hesitates a moment, and then opens it again.

You'll be all right? Shall I wait for you? I mean, you can find your way back, can you? It's the door immediately opposite, not the one round to the left. That's the kitchen.

Stephen *closes the door reluctantly again. He goes to the kitchen door to listen. Apparently reassured, he hurries back to the living-room, resuming his story to the occupants as he enters.*

Yes, so anyway, the upshot of it was that Nicholas had to go to the Ambassador's dressed as a horse . . . !

He closes the door behind him. At once **Alex** *reappears from the corridor door*

Alex	It's locked!

He realises that **Stephen** *has disappeared.*

Oh . . .

He looks round the room in despair, and spots a vase of flowers. He crosses to it, looks round the room to make sure no one is coming, then takes the flowers out and retires with the vase behind the window curtains. At once the lavatory flushes off, and **Barney** *comes back through the corridor door. He goes to the kitchen door, then hesitates.*

Barney   Just a moment. What was I going to do? Oh, find poor old Stephen and Jo.

He crosses to the living-room.

Come out of there! No need to hide from me!
Alex   (*putting his head round the curtain*) Sorry! I'm just in the middle of something.

Barney *stops and gazes at* **Alex** *in astonishment.* **Alex** *disappears again.*

Barney   So they have got an au pair girl after all!

He pulls the curtain back and reveals **Alex**.

Barney   Hello!
Alex   Oh . . . hi . . .
Barney   What's your name, then?
Alex   Er . . . Alex . . .
Barney   Alex. That's a very pretty name.
Alex   Oh . . . glad you like it . . .

He moves towards the living-room door.

Barney   Well, don't rush off, Alex, now you're here. Stay and talk for a bit – I'm on my own.
Alex   Oh . . . Right . . .
Barney   Doesn't it get you down, looking after the children all the time?
Alex   The kids? No . . . I don't get much trouble. There's the usual business about, you know, pot.

Barney	They still use the pot, do they?
Alex	Oh, yeah, most of them.
Barney	That must make a lot of extra work for you.
Alex	Oh, I just try to stop them getting busted.
Barney	The pots?
Alex	The kids. I mean, you know, I try to sort of keep the fuzz off their necks as much as possible.
Barney	That's a problem, is it, the fuzz on their necks?
Alex	Oh, you get the fuzz round, you know, twice a night, sometimes.
Barney	It's funny, Alex – I feel I can talk to you. I feel we somehow understand each other. Do you feel that?
Alex	(*Politely*) Oh . . . well . . . you know. . .
Barney	(*Putting his arm around* **Alex**) I mean, I expect I seem rather old to you, don't I?
Alex	No, no . . .
Barney	You're probably thinking, who is this terrible dirty old man, coming and putting his arm round me like this?
Alex	No, I mean, you've got to be, you know, sort of open-minded about this kind of thing, haven't you?
Barney	I expect you're wondering if I'm married.
Alex	No, honestly, I'm not wondering anything . . .
Barney	Well, I wouldn't tell this to anyone else, Alex, but she's walked out on me. My wife. Without so much as a by-your-leave. One moment she was there, and the next – woof! – she was gone. But do you know who she's gone off with? She's gone off with someone in ear-rings! What do you think of that?
Alex	(*obviously unable to decide what he is supposed to think of this*) Oh . . . well . . .
Barney	I mean, she used to try and tell me I was a bit obsessional. But she! – She's a complete raving neurotic! You ought to meet her, Alex!
Alex	Yes, well, there's this bird I'm, you know, going around with at the moment . . .
Barney	You . . . go around with birds, too, do you, Alex?
Alex	Yeah . . . I mean, birds are more, you know, my thing. I mean, no offence . . .
Barney	No, I admire you for it, Alex! It's this tremendous broad-mindedness, this wonderful openness to experience that

	my generation lacks. I mean, take my wife. She's just a mass of repressions and inhibitions – that's why she's so neurotic.
Alex	Yes, well, this bird's like that. This bird I'm, you know, going around with. Thinks everyone's getting at her all the time.
Barney	My wife – exactly the same!
Alex	Oh, they're all the same, in my opinion.
Barney	I mean, we'd go out to dinner somewhere, and I'd put my arm round someone I'd known for donkey's years – just like I'm doing now, just the same, nothing more in it than that – and I'd look round, and my wife would have disappeared. And do you know where she'd be?
Alex	In the bathroom, crying her eyes out.
Barney	(*agreeing, wonderingly*) In the bathroom, crying her eyes out!
Alex	I mean, so *jealous* . . . !
Barney	My God, it's marvellous meeting someone who *understands* like this!
Alex	It's fantastic being able to, you know, sort of get it off your chest, at last, isn't it? I mean, this bird I'm talking about . . .
Barney	(*interrupting*) Would you like a drink, Alex? I've got a drop of Scotch out here. Yes, go on . . .

He goes into the kitchen. **Alex** *follows him as far as the door, and stands talking there as a hand first holds up the bottle of whisky, then a moment later proffers a full glass.*

Alex	I mean, I can see why she's so, you know, hung up. She's married to this bloke who's even nuttier than she is . . . Thanks . . . They'd go out to a party, or something, and the first thing she knew she'd find him out in the kitchen, feeling up the bird who was giving the party and telling her that it was her he'd really meant to marry all the time. Well, it would make anyone insecure, wouldn't it? And you know what he did once . . . ?

The hand reappears holding a second glass of whisky, clinks it against his, and disappears. **Alex** *raises his glass.*

The same to you.

He drinks down the whisky.

He got so, you know, stoned, he went out to the kitchen and started feeling up the bird's husband by mistake, and telling *him* the tale!

The arm appears and ushers him into the kitchen. The door closes. At once the living-room door opens and **Stephen** *comes out, still holding the bottle of wine, and addressing the occupants.*

Stephen . . . but above all, surely, it's a question of setting the present economic crisis within the context of European cultural structure . . .

He closes the door, and looks anxiously round the room, calling in a stage whisper.

Alex . . . ? Alex . . . !

He crosses to the corridor door, and calls off.

Alex! Are you all right!

There being no answer, he goes out to investigate, and returns an instant later, baffled. He notices that the curtain is disarranged, crosses to it, and finds the vase behind. Frowning, he replaces the flowers. As he does do, the kitchen door opens, and the broken remains of the dicky dining-chair are thrown out. He spins round, and picks the chair up.

Barney! What have you done with this chair?

He tries to open the kitchen door, but it is locked.

Barney! Barney . . . ? What's happening? Why won't this door open? Why have you locked the door, Barney? And what have you been doing to this chair! All right, the leg was loose – but to get it into this condition you'd have needed two people sitting on it or something . . . !

The implication of his words strikes him, he turns back to the door.

Barney . . . ! *Barney* . . . !

The living-room door opens, and **Bee** *enters. She is wearing some astonishing minimal see-through type of outfit, more suitable to someone ten years younger.*

Bee	(*anxiously*) Stephen . . .
Stephen	(*whirling round, and attempting to hide the very existence of the kitchen door*) Bee!
Bee	Where's Alex?
Stephen	I'm not quite sure, Bee. Around somewhere.
Bee	Perhaps he's in the kitchen . . .
Stephen	(*guarding it*) No, no, no – I've looked. There's no one there. He went to the loo, originally.
Bee	He can't still be in the loo, can he?
Stephen	(*urging her*) Why don't you just go and look?
Bee	I mean, I don't want to fuss. He can't stand me fussing.
Stephen	But all the same . . .
Bee	All the same, if something had happened to him . ., .
Stephen	(*holding the corridor door open for her*) First on the left, second on the right.
Bee	Oh, I expect he got bored and went home.
Stephen	(*seizing on this explanation with relief*) Yes, he did!
Bee	(*surprised*) He did?
Stephen	Of course he did! I forgot to tell you. He said he had a headache, so he was going home. He just slipped quietly out the back so as not to break up the party. How stupid of me to forget!

Bee *gazes at him for a moment, and then suddenly gives a loud despairing wail and bursts into tears.*

What? What is it, Bee? What's the matter?

He puts a baffled protecting arm around her, looking back anxiously over his shoulder at the kitchen. She seizes him gratefully and cries into his chest.

Sh, Bee! What is it?

Bee   Don't you see? He's left me!

Stephen   Left you?

Bee   I *knew* he would! I *knew* it couldn't last!

Stephen   He hasn't left you, Bee! He's just gone home with a headache!

Bee   Headache!

Stephen   He said he'd ring you tomorrow.

*But this makes **Bee** give a cry of fresh pain, and weep more bitterly still.*

No, he said he'd ring you *tonight* . . .

But this makes it worse still.

He's going to ring you the moment you get in! So you see he hasn't left you, has he, Bee!

Bee   (*bitterly*) He wouldn't have to ring me if he hadn't moved out, would he?

She wails more loudly than ever.

Stephen   No, well, I've got that wrong.

He looks round anxiously at the kitchen door.

I didn't mean he was going to *ring* you, exactly. I meant . . .

Bee   Oh, shut up, Stephen! You're just making it worse!

Stephen   No, what I meant was . . .

Bee   Oh, Stephen! You're the only friend I've got left in the world! Don't you leave me!

Stephen   No, I won't but . . .

Bee   Alex has walked out on me. Barney hates me. All my friends have turned against me because of Alex. All Alex's friends treat me as if I were his mother. Jo's afraid I'll have an affair with you next . . . You're the only person left, Stephen! I've always felt you were the one man I could really talk to. If only we'd met earlier it could all have been so simple!

She embraces him hysterically. He looks wildly from door to door, uncertain as to which he would less welcome intervention from.

Stephen	Sh! Sh! Calm down now!
Bee	Oh, Stephen!
Stephen	(*disengaging himself with difficulty*) Now, you just wait here . . . and I'll go and fetch you a nice stiff calming drink . . .
Bee	(*seizing him again*) Don't leave me!
Stephen	I shan't be a minute . . . You just sit down and relax . . .

He attempts to set the broken chair for her, then realises what he is doing and picks it up again.

I mean, you just stand up and relax . . .

He goes through the living-room door, resuming his conversation with the occupants as he does so.

. . . and, of course, of setting European cultural structure within the context of the economic crisis . . .

He disappears and shuts the door. At the sight of the door shutting **Bee** *gives way to a new burst of despair.*

Bee	Now they've all gone! They've all left me! I've no one to turn to!

She in fact turns towards the kitchen door, and leans against it in melodramatic despair, in the attitude of Love Locked Out.

No one! No one!

Suddenly she stops crying and lifts her hand from the door. She listens, frowning, then puts her ear to the door and listens again, puzzled.

Alex! That's Alex's voice!

Bee *turns away from the door, opens her handbag and hastily begins to refurbish her appearance.*

Bee   Oh God! Mustn't let him see I was worried . . . Cheerful smile, knew he was there all the time . . .

As she finishes this task the door opens, and **Barney** *comes thoughtfully out. She closes her bag and turns to him, smiling.*

     Alex!

Barney   (*putting his arm round her confidentially*) Jo, there's something I think you ought to know about that *au pair* girl of yours . . .

His voice dies away as he gets his gaze properly focused on her. She is staring at him, transfixed with astonishment.

     Bee!

Bee   Barney!

For a moment they just stare at each other, still embraced. Then, abruptly, **Bee** *breaks away and opens the kitchen door to see who is inside. Hastily* **Barney** *pulls it shut again.*

Barney   Friend of mine, that's all.
Bee   You and Alex . . . ?
Barney   We were just having a friendly conversation – nothing more to it.
Bee   (*wildly*) You and Alex – having a friendly conversation? It's a conspiracy! Getting together behind my back!

She turns and rushes off, weeping, through the corridor door.

Barney   (*following her as far as the door*) No, Bee, listen . . . Stop . . . !

He is going to pursue her further, but at that moment the kitchen door opens. He runs back to it.

Now you keep out of this! You've caused enough trouble already!

He puts his hand round the door and takes the key out of the lock on the other side

Au pair girls! My God, I knew young people were confused, but I didn't know the rot had gone this far!

He slams the door shut and locks it. Then, pocketing the key, he runs back to the corridor door.

Bee! Listen! Let me explain . . . !

He seizes the handle of the corridor door and pushes, assuming in his anxiety that it opens the same way as the kitchen door. But it doesn't. He calls imperiously.

Open the door! Come on, open the door! *Open this door!*

He hammers on it, then suddenly drops his commanding manner, and becomes pleading instead.

Look, Bee, it's all a misunderstanding! You looking in there, you thought it was the *au pair* girl, didn't you! I thought it was the *au pair* girl! But listen, Bee, you open this door and I'll tell you an astonishing fact . . . Bee . . . !

He turns away from the door for a moment, amazed at himself.

Though why the hell I should be excusing myself to her . . . !

He addresses himself furiously to the door again, hammering and shouting.

Open this door at once! I know what you're doing – you

needn't think I don't! You're in the bathroom, having a good old weep!

Girl Child's Voice   (*calling from off*) Mummy! Mummy! There's a lady crying in the bathroom!

Barney   (*shouting at the top of his voice*) Look, *stop* crying in the bathroom, and come down and open this door!

He rains a frustrated fusillade of blows upon the door, then stops, realising that someone else somewhere is hammering on a door. He runs furiously across to the kitchen, and shouts through the closed door.

Stop that noise at once! I can scarcely hear myself knock!

There is another salvo of bangs from the kitchen, to which he bangs furiously back.

One more bang out of you, my girl, and I'll put the police on to you, my lad!

He runs furiously back to the corridor and thunders on that one again.

Come downstairs this instant and open the door!

Barney *shouts and thunders,* **Alex** *thunders too. There is a sudden brief lull, during which the living-room door opens, and* **Jo** *enters, holding a nice stiff calming drink, and talking back over her shoulder to the occupants of the living room.*

Jo   . . . in which case, so much for European cultural structure . . . !

She closes the door.

Barney   (*to* **Jo** *in furious explanation*) She's in the bathroom, weeping!

Jo   Stephen said she needed a stiff drink . . .

Barney   She'll need more than a stiff drink if I ever get my hands on her!

He whirls back upon the door, pounding on it and shouting at the top of his voice.

Jo	Can't you understand? I'm trying to tell you I love you!
Barney	Why don't you go up and tell her at slightly closer range?
	Because the little bitch has locked the door!

He hurls his weight against it to demonstrate.

Jo	It opens this way.
Barney	(*almost too furious to comprehend*) What?
Jo	Pull it.

He pulls violently. It opens without let or hindrance, sending him straight back into the room. As he picks himself up there is another salvo of knocking from the kitchen.

	What's that?
Barney	That's your friend Alex. I've locked him in the kitchen pending his arrest on a variety of serious charges . . . All *right!* I'm coming . . . !

He rushes out through the corridor door. There is the noise of heavy feet thundering up the stairs, then of rending wood, then of glass objects smashing. Calmly, **Jo** *goes over to the corridor door.*

Boy Child's Voice	(*calling from off*) Mummy! *Mummy!* There's a lady and a man fighting in the bathroom!
Jo	Go to *sleep*, dear! I don't want to hear another sound out of you two – you know we've got people to dinner.

With philosophical calm **Jo** *closes the door, to deaden the continuing noise. There is another salvo of blows from the kitchen. She raises her eyebrows wearily, notices the nice stiff calming drink still in her hand, and drinks it down stoically. As she finishes it, the living-room door opens, and* **Stephen** *creeps quietly out, looking anxiously back over his shoulder and smiling* *benignly. He shuts the door behind him.* **Jo** *reports the situation to him with calm detachment.*

Barney and Bee are fighting in the bathroom. Alex and the rest of the dinner are locked in the kitchen. The children are awake.

Stephen   David and Doris are asleep.

Jo   John and Laura. Are you sure?

Stephen   They hadn't said anything for quite a while. I don't know whether you'd noticed.

Jo *opens the living-room door. She and* **Stephen** *both gaze off at* **John** *and* **Laura.** *Bursts of noise from the bathroom and kitchen continue intermittently.*

It was the economic crisis that finished them, I think.

Jo   I knew we should have kept off politics.

Stephen   They look quite peaceful.

Jo   I *think* they quite enjoyed the evening, didn't they?

Stephen   Oh, I think everyone did, all things considered.

Jo   I think it all went off reasonably well.

Stephen   Jo, I'm sorry I shouted at you earlier.

Jo   I lost my temper. It always gets a bit tense when people are coming to dinner. You always think everything's going to go wrong.

Stephen   It seems so ridiculous afterwards. You can't think what you were so worried about.

Somewhere a window is smashed.

Jo   (*with relief*) Anyway, that's four people we owed dinner to knocked off.

Stephen   Five!

Jo   Yes! The only trouble is we haven't had anything to eat ourselves. I'm starving.

Stephen   So am I. Come on – let's nip round the corner and have a plate of fish and chips.

They creep out through the living-room.

Value for Money

Fellow Guest   Oh, you live in the North, do you? How super.
What fun. You don't by any chance know the
Uzzards? They live in the North somewhere. He's
in some terrific chemical thing up there, and she's
hideously pretty. I mean, I hardly know them, but I do
remember someone saying they lived up in that part
of the world. You *must* meet them, they're *frightful*
sweeties. Well, I say, they're up in the North, but of
course at the moment they aren't because he's doing
. . . what is he doing? How is it that one can never
remember what people are doing? I think he's doing
five years. I *think* I'm right in saying five. There was
some terrible confusion about some money thing he
was mixed up with. Such a pity, because he's such
good value. And she's so madly sensible about it all.
And the absolutely unforgivably ghastly thing is that
I've forgotten what she's doing, but I think what
she's doing is life. There was some kind of dreadful
muddle about her au pair getting sort of murdered.
Such rotten luck. And of course just when she needed
the girl most! Maddening when you get a good one,
and off she goes. Because the tragic thing was, the
girl was an absolute marvel. I think that's why David
got involved in this terrible confusion about the
money thing. I *think* so. There was some ghastly mix-
up over sort of fur-coats and abortion sort of things. I
think that was it. Then Sue heard that David had got
involved in this muddle about the money thing and
she thought, wow, and *she* got into this muddle about
the murder thing. So absolutely awful when everyone
involved is so awfully nice. And such killingly good
value. But you've never met them? And now they're
not in the North any more! How sickening. Such a
dreadful waste, somehow. No, I mean of the North.
Still, I get the impression it's frightful fun living
up there.

The Property Speculators

Mother	What a lucky old woman I am! Having three sons so good to me! You know how much I appreciate your finding the time to take me for a run in the motor like this.
John	You just sit back and enjoy the view, Mother. What do you reckon that one is, then, Ralph?
Ralph	The one with the crazy-paving washdown? Oh, two hundred John, at least.
John	Two hundred? Two hundred and fifty more likely.
Howard	What about that one there, with all the wrought iron on the sun lounge?
Ralhp	Must be getting on for two-fifty as well, Howard.
John	Nearer three hundred, I'd say. I mean, you know where we are – the Wroxtead Valley estate.
Howard	Oh, it's pricey round here all right. I'm not denying it.
Ralph	Especially up this end. Aren't we just coming out at that five-way junction on the Surley by-pass?
John	That's right. By that new roadhouse there, the Olde Shippe.
Ralph	Hey, look at that one then! With the Jag outside!
John	I'll tell you what, Ralph. I bet that's three-fifty.
Mother	Three-fifty what, dear?
Howard	The HOUSE, Mother. The house is three-fifty.
John	Here's the by-pass then. Now where?
Ralph	How about cutting down Hatcham Park Road to North Sudstow? We could try out the new underpass in Sudstow Village on the way back.
John	Fair enough.
Mother	Talking about houses reminds me of a house your grandfather's brother Tom once owned. It was somewhere overlooking the river in Chelsea, and Whistler was supposed to have . . .
John	Yes, but who wants to live in the middle of London, Mother? Pricey round here, you know, Ralph, in Hatcham Park.
Ralph	Pretty pricey.

John	I don't know what one of these houses would cost you.
Howard	Oh, a packet, John, a real packet.
Ralph	I mean, I know a chap in the office – nice chap, got a couple of kids, one of them suffers rather badly from asthma – and his brother-in-law bought, not one of these houses, but one of those big ones up by the cemetery at Upsome. You know where I mean? Well, that cost him close on two hundred thousand, and it wasn't anything like one of these. And that was five years ago, when prices just weren't comparable.
John	I know. I know.
Ralph	What one of these would cost you I don't know.
Mother	Ralph was always the clever one.
Howard	This is more or less North Sudstow here.
John	Not cheap here, you know.
Howard	Quite pricey, by the look of it. What would you say that one with the Spanish-type porch would cost?
John	Must be three hundred thousand at the very least, mustn't it?
Ralph	What about that new split-level ranch house, then, with the latticed dormer windows? Stop for a moment, John, and let's have a look at it.
Mother	Are we going for a walk?
John	No, no Mother. Just you sit back and admire the scenery. Shall I tell you what I think, Ralph? This may surprise you, Ralph, but it's really and truly what I think –
Howard	Go on.
John	Three-fifty.
Ralph	Three-fifty? You may be right at that. I was going to say three, three-twenty.
John	Three-fifty. Ah well, let's press on.
Mother	Wouldn't it be nice if one day we could go out into the country on one of these runs? But then I suppose there's no country left these days?
John	Country, Mother? This *is* the country. We're in the Green Belt here.
Howard	Can't you see the grass verges, Mother?
Ralph	Her eyesight's going, you know.
John	Know this road we're joining now? The Vale, Sudstow.

You could have got one of these houses here for a song ten years ago. They couldn't give them away.

Howard   Fantastic, isn't it? Some of these people must have mopped up three or four hundred per cent profit.

Ralph   Does something to you to think about it, doesn't it?

Howard   Beats me the way human beings carry on about things like houses. You'd think they'd have other things to think about.

John   Now I've got a real surprise for you. It's a little road I discovered the other day by pure accident. This next one on the right – Bolderwood Avenue. Take a look at it. They don't make them much pricier than this.

Howard   Very pricey indeed, John.

Ralph   You certainly know how to pick them.

Howard   Look at that one with the weather-boarding on the gables! I should think the garages alone must have cost fifty thousand!

Ralph   It's marvellous what you can spend, isn't it, when you come down to it?

Howard   What do you think these places would fetch: Half a million?

Ralph   Three-quarters.

Howard   Three-quarters plus.

John   It'd be wrong to guess, Howard. There are some things in life you can't reckon in figures alone.

Howard   You're right there.

Ralph   Ah, it's a real tonic just to look at them.

John   Well then, home, James.

Mother   It *is* good of you boys to bother with me, taking me out to see the world like this. It's a pleasure just to listen to you – my word, how you do appreciate everything you set your eyes on!

Who Do You Think You Are?

Woman	(*carrying a tray with a cup of tea on it*) Excuse me, is this seat . . . ?
Man	No, no.

She sits down and sips her tea.

	Usually in here around this time, aren't you?
Woman	Come in about quarter to six, ten to six, usually.
Man	Yes, I'm usually in here around this time. Have a cup of tea before I go home. Calm down.
Woman	I need my cup of tea today.
Man	One of those days?
Woman	Terrible.
Man	Should have seen mine. I say you should have seen *my* day!
Woman	Some people seem to think if you work in a shop you're just there to lick their boots.
Man	Oh, that sort.
Woman	Treat you like dirt. Think they're the Lord High Executioner.
Man	You should have my job.
Woman	'Haven't got it in stock?' 'I'm sorry, Madam.' 'This is disgusting. I shall write to the Managing Director and complain.' 'Yes, Madam.'
Man	I say, you should have my job.
Woman	They just want someone to take it out on.
Man	They ring me up. Why haven't the men turned up to repair the central heating? Half the time they've been, and there was no one there.
Woman	They really make me sick.
Man	Get quite nasty, some of them. You know, sarcastic. It's the phone that does it. You're just a voice to them. They wouldn't dare say it to your face.
Woman	A man rang up today. Complained he'd had to wait half an hour to be served.
Man	I had a woman on the phone this afternoon. Told

me she was going to ring the Chairman at home to
complain.

Woman   Then he waxed very sarcastic. Wanted to know if he'd get
a prize to mark the occasion. Nothing to do with me – I
hadn't even been there! I was sitting at home waiting for
the man to come and mend my washing-machine!

Man   It's nice when you have a chance to get your own back,
though. I rang up some place today and really gave some
old cow what-for. Did the old heart good, I can tell
you. Well, I'd stood in this shop waiting half-an-hour to
be served!

Woman   Yes, I rang this firm up when I got to work and really let
this fellow have it. Told him I'd ring their Chairman at
home. That soon shut him up.

Man   I said, 'Am I by any chance entitled to some kind of cup or
medal as a reward for long service?'

Woman   What I can't bear is when they try and fob you off by
coming over all greasy and humble.

Man   Oh, that sort! This woman was like that.

Woman   So was this man. Ugh! Some people!

Man   Some right ones around, aren't there?

Woman   Nice to come in here and find there's still someone human
left in the world.

Head to Head

A Head of State   . . . gives me great pleasure to be here – to see
your beautiful and historic country for myself,
and to bring greetings from my people across the
sea to the people of Fandangia.

And here I must say what especial pleasure
it gives me to be in Fandangia as the guest of
President Goizi.

Applause.

In the hearts and in the affections of my
countrymen, President Goizi will always hold
a special place. We know how faithfully he
has served Fandangia. We have watched him
at the helm through times that have not always
been easy, amidst the perilous shoals of our
world today.

I may say that I had the privilege and good
fortune to meet the previous President, President
Fasces. It seems only yesterday that I was
paying tribute to him at a not entirely dissimilar
occasion. But it was in fact the day before
yesterday, and since his tragic death early this
morning President Goizi has shown himself in
every way a worthy successor.

But we, in our country, have special reason
for the affection in which we hold President
Goizi. For we know that the warm and friendly
relations that exist between our two nations
today are due in no small measure to his interest
and to his unremitting efforts. It is perhaps
not out of place to recall that President Goizi
has visited us. He has seen us at work and
play. He has tasted a sample of our national
cooking.

Laughter

. . . – and, I am assured, pronounced it not greatly inferior to Fandangian cooking.

Laughter.

He has watched our national game.

Laughter.

– and, I believe, declared himself mystified by it.

Loud laughter.

In short, we know that he has seen us at first hand, in times that have not always been easy, and observed how we have faced the perils that confront every nation in the world today. It is bonds like these that unite our two peoples.

Applause.

But we must not let our sense of history make us unaware of the changing world in which we live. We must not let our regard for tradition, and for the preservation of what is best in our way of life – important as these things are – blind us to the events which are taking place about us. And at this point it is perhaps not inappropriate that I should say how particularly pleased I am to find myself in Fandangia as the guest of President Bombardos.

Applause.

In terms of the time in which these things are measured, it might perhaps be said that President Bombardos has not been responsible for guiding Fandangia'a destinies for very long. But already,

since he took over the duties which were so
unexpectedly thrust upon him after the sudden
retirement for health reasons of his predecessor,
President Goizi, this evening, he has proved
himself to be a worthy successor.

He has brought Fandangia through times
which for all of us have not been without their
difficulties. It is perhaps scarcely an exaggeration
to say that he has made this nation what it is at
the moment. And in the hearts and minds of my
countrymen, President Bombardos will always
be assured of a special place. Already we have
come to learn that in President Bombardos we
have a true friend. I believe that it is not entirely
inappropriate to recollect that he has spent
some time among our people. One of his special
concerns was to study our police forces – which
he was kind enough to say were 'wonderful'.

Laughter.

I believe he also had a taste of our weather

Laughter.

though there is no record of his saying the same
thing about that.

Loud laughter.

In other words, President Bombardos has
seen us as we are, looked at the best and worst
in our nation, and, as we like to think, come to
understand us. For us, President Bombardos *is*
Fandangia.

Prolonged applause.

But I should not like you to think that
this close and friendly interest in every last

development is not fully reciprocated. I cannot therefore finish without paying personal tribute to the President of the Fandangian Republic, President Goizi, who, with the exception of a brief interregnum very recently, has guided your destinies for so long . . .

Glycerine

Husband	(*enters*) I've put the leftovers on the side. I don't know what you want to do with them . . . I said, I've put the leftovers on the side.
Wife	(*looks up for an instant from the television screen*) On the side. Right.
Husband	(*sits down*) What's this then? What have you got yourself?
Wife	(*absorbed*) I don't know. Some historical thing.
Husband	What's it about?
Wife	(*sighing*) He's in love with her, only she doesn't . . . Tch . . .
Husband	Only she doesn't what?
Wife	I don't know . . . She's . . . It's all in days gone by . . .
Husband	Who's *that*?
Wife	I think he just . . . lives there.
Husband	Lives where?
Wife	There.
Husband	(*impatiently*) Where's the paper? I can't stand not knowing what I'm looking at.
Wife	Well, he's the one we saw in that other thing. The thing about the man who was going to . . . I don't know . . . blow something up, wasn't he? Only they found out about it somehow, and . . . I don't know . . . It all took place abroad somewhere.
Husband	'9.20 – Party Political Broadcast.'
Wife	That's yesterday's.
Husband	Why have we *never* got today's paper? What do you do with it? You know I hate sitting here not knowing what I'm looking at.
Wife	Anyway, she's the one who's married to that man.
Husband	Married to that man? What man? Which man?
Wife	That man in that thing we saw about . . . whatever it was . . .
Husband	Oh, blimey!
Wife	They can't have children. I saw it in the paper. They've adopted two little boys . . . They say she's got a lovely

home . . . four-poster bed . . . antique commodes . . . I don't know . . .

Husband *Now* what's happening? She's on a ship now! A moment ago she was in prison! What's going on?

Wife She's on her way to find . . . the other one.

Husband What other one?

Wife The one that's always eating toffees.

Husband Toffees? Toffees hadn't been invented then!

Wife In that commercial.

Husband You sit in front of that set in a trance. Do you know that? You haven't the slightest idea what's happening in front of your eyes . . .

She smiles.

What was that? I missed that. What did he say?

Wife (*sighs*) I don't know. Something about I prithee something.

Husband You don't even know what they're saying!

Wife I can't *hear* what they're saying with you going jabber jabber all the time, who's this, who's that?

Husband If you don't know what he said, what are you sniggering at it for? Honestly, you let that television set turn you into a moron. I mean, I'm not anti-television. Far from it. Television can educate and stimulate the mind – if you watch it *actively*. If you *discuss* what you're watching and really try to . . . He'll get his bloody head chopped off if he leaves it there . . .

Wife Tch.

Husband I told you . . . I mean, if you took an interest in how it's done. For instance, *that*. Do you know how they do her tears? You don't think she can just cry to order?

She discreetly sheds a few tears herself.

That's glycerine. Little drops of glycerine running down her face. Exactly the same as that stuff in the bathroom cabinet that you put on your hands in winter. Combined with nitrogen it forms nitro-glycerine, the well-known explosive. I mean, if you had a critical attitude. If you just asked yourself whether you're really enjoying it. Are you enjoying *this*?

Wife   (*sniffing*) I don't know. I'm just watching it, that's all.
Husband Well. *think*, then! Make an effort for once! Use your brain! That's what God gave it to you for . . . !

The words trail away. He gazes at the screen, hypnotised. So does his wife, her tears forgotten. There is a long silence.

Wife   Tch.
Husband Tch.

Then suddenly they both relax, and move uncomfortably about in their chairs.

That's what you should be asking yourself – why they put all this sex in that no one wants to watch.

A Pleasure Shared

Fellow Guest   Do you spit? No? You don't mind if I do, though . . .
Khhghm . . . Hold on – can you see a spittoon
on the table anywhere . . . ? Never mind. Sit
down, sit down! I can use my empty soup-bowl.
Khhghm – *thpp!*

My God, that's better. No, I've been sitting here
all the way through the first course just dying for
one. Iron self-control, but I do think it's rather
bad manners to spit while one's eating. I mean, at
a dinner-party like this. Your mouth is full of the
hostess's soup, and suddenly , . . kkhghm – *thpp!*

You *have* finished yourself, haven't you? You
haven't! I'm so sorry . . . Oh, you don't want
the rest.

Very nice of you not to . . . khhghm – *thpp!* . . .
not to mind. One has to be so careful these days
not to offend people's prejudices. I always ask first,
of course. People never raise any objection, in my
experience. In fact they usually never say anything
at all. They generally do what you did – smile rather
charmingly and kind of wave their hand about. Quite
surprised even to be asked, I think, most of them.

Khhghm . . . Where's the soup-bowl gone . . . ?
No, no – sit down! Don't keep jumping up! I'll use
yours! You did say you'd finished . . . ? *Thpp!*

I'm glad you're not one of these hysterical people
who try to stop other people enjoying themselves.
It's so one-sided. I don't try to stop anyone *not*
spitting over me! In fact this is something I feel
rather strongly about. People used to spit all the
time in the good old days, and no one so much as
raised an eyebrow. Spittoons everywhere you went
– sawdust on the floor. It was only about fifty years
ago, you know, that all this anti-spitting nonsense
started. Suddenly everyone went mad. Notices up in

the buses – 'No spitting. Penalty £5'. And before we knew what had happened we'd lost another of our ancient liberties.

So quite honestly, I . . . Khhghm . . . Oh, they've taken the soup-bowls away . . . No, no stay right where you are! *Thpp.* . . ! Keeps the moth out of the tablecloth . . . Yes, I spit very largely as a matter of principle.

And I hawk. As you can hear. Khhghm . . . !
In fact I hawk *deeply*, also as a matter of principle. *Khhhhhghhhhm* . . . ! Because I believe that if you're going to spit you might as well get the full benefit of it, and shift the entire contents of your lungs out into the atmosphere. Why keep all that stuff festering inside you, when you could so easily . . . Khhghm – *thpp*! . . . spread it around a bit . . . ?

Didn't spit in your face then, did I? Hold on – I think I did! I'm sorry. I'll just give it a wipe with the corner of the tablecloth . . . Come back, come back! The tablecloth's perfectly . . . no, sorry, hold on, I'll try another bit . . . There we are. It's very nice of you to go on smiling about it, but I know even the most broad-minded non-spitters sometimes feel a little sensitive about getting a faceful of the stuff.

Anyway, point taken! I'll be very careful henceforth to turn my head aside, look, and . . . Khhghm – *thpp*! . . . spit in your very lovely hair, or down your very charming dress.

Why don't I sit a little closer? There . . . It's the alluring way you're . . . Khhghm – *thpp*! . . . wriggling around! I beg your pardon . . . ? It tickles? What tickles . . . ? You mean it ran down inside your dress? It gets everywhere, doesn't it! Anyway, don't worry. Just hang your underwear up in some airy place when you get home tonight, and it'll be dry in no time.

Look, you wouldn't mind, would you, if . . . No, come here! Don't lean away! I'm trying to whisper a few private words in your ear. You wouldn't mind, would you, if I gave you a ring

some time? I thought perhaps you might like to
come round one evening. I could give you a quiet
spot of . . . Khhghm – *thpp*! Or we might go out
and do something a little more exciting. I don't
know. Maybe – Khhghhkhkhkhm – *thppshmk*!

You keep shaking your head. Did you get some
in your ear? Don't worry – it's not as if you were
inhaling it . . . What? Oh, you're saying no? I see. I
see. You're not somehow offended because you got
a tiny bit in your eye . . . ? I thought so! I *thought*
that smile of yours was beginning to get a little fixed.
My God! I did *ask*, if you remember. I did ask if you
minded!

So you're one of these anti-spitting fanatics, are
you? I'm not allowed to spit – is that what you're
telling me? – but it's perfectly all right for you to go
round leaning away from people, and grinning that
ghastly glassy grin at them.

God, the *intolerance* of you lot! It makes me want
to . . . Well, I'll tell you what it makes me want to
do. It makes me want to khhhhhhghhhhhm – Oh,
and here's the next course. I'll put that one back
for later.

Sons and Customers

Mother Chocolates! Well, that *is* kind of you, Ralph. What with flowers from you, John, and bath salts from you, Howard, and you all three driving down to see me like this, I *am* having a lovely birthday! You shouldn't have bothered, you know. I'm sure you've all got much more important things to think about.

Ralph That's all right, Mother – you only get a birthday once a year, you know. Incidentally, John, do you know where I bought those chocolates? Stanmores in Creese End Broadway.

John I thought you always bought your sweets and cigarettes in that branch of Goodmans opposite Wemblemore tube station?

Ralph I used to. But I changed to Stanmores.

Howard Well, you surprise me, Ralph. I thought you swore by Goodmans.

Ralph I did. But do you know, I think you get better service at Stanmores. I really do.

John That's you all over, Ralph – chopping and changing until you find something that really suits you.

Mother Ralph always was the adventurous one.

John I admire you for it, Ralph. But I couldn't do it myself. I mean, those flowers – I bought them at Gossards in Broylesden High Street. Now I've been buying flowers at Gossards for 15 years or more.

Ralph I know you have, John, I know you have.

John They know me there. They know my name, they know my children's names, they know the sort of flowers I like. Well, they *know* me.

Howard There *is* such a thing as loyalty, isn't there, after all? Look at me. I've been taking my car into the Upsome branch of Qualitimotors for 10 years now. They know me. They know the car.

John You know they care about you. You know you're someone to them.

Howard I always feels they're genuinely pleased to see me in

Qualitimotors. And not just me. They're pleased to see the car.

John   I mean, today for instance. I was going to buy the carnations at five pounds a dozen. But the manager said to me, he said: 'Frankly, Mr Tooting, they're not worth it.' I mean, he was quite frank with me. 'They're not worth the money, Mr Tooting,' he said. 'I know you, Mr Tooting, and if I were you I'd have the chrysanths at 50p each and put the change in my pocket.'

Ralph   Oh, I agree. I agree.

John   They know I won't stand any nonsense.

Mother   When it comes to nonsense, a very strange thing happened to me once in a shop in Singapore.

John   You just sit back and enjoy yourself, Mother. It's your birthday, remember.

Ralph   No, as I was saying, John, I agree with you. Take me now. I get my wines and spirits from a little man in Dorris Hill.

Howard   'Simon the Cellarer' in Manor Park Road, isn't it?

Ralph   That's right. Run by a chap called Nuthall. Been dealing with him for donkey's years now, and when it comes to wines, well, I trust his judgement. 'You know, Mr Tooting,' he said to me once, 'I never need to ask you – I know it's not the cheap stuff you'll be wanting.' Proper character, old Nuthall. And if he gets the orders mixed up he'll always take it back without any argument.

Howard   It's the same with me at Qualitimotors. I always deal with the Service Manager himself, of course.

John   Yes, it's the manager who always serves me at Gossards.

Howard   'Hello, Mr Tooting,' he says when I go in. 'The old clutch playing up again?' And ready to oblige! Well, I've taken the same repair on the clutch back six times to get it right without anyone saying a word.

John   Mark you, you pay for it.

Ralph   Oh, of course you do. But then you and I expect to pay a bit over the odds. Some people are happy to buy stuff on the cheap, and good luck to them. But you and I have been brought up differently.

Howard   Though it's not just a matter of money, of course. I mean, you go into Qualitimotors in a Jag, flashing a roll of notes, and I don't suppose they'd reckon much to you. But you go in and say I sent you and I think you can be pretty sure they'll look after you all right.

Ralph   If it comes to that, I think you'll find my name's a pretty good passport anywhere along Creese End or Dorris Hill.

Howard   Well, in Higgins and Dickens you've only to mention my name and they'll give you the freedom of the shop.

John   I'm not exaggerating, Howard, but if I so much as raised an eyebrow in Higgins and Dickens they'd get down on their hands and knees and clean my boots.

Ralph   Without a word of a lie, John, I could walk down Creese End Broadway tomorrow and have my boots *licked* clean by the manager of every quality shop in turn.

John   Mark you, I think we've a right to it. I think I can say in all honesty I'm a pretty good customer of Higgins and Dickens.

Howard   Yes, we're all pretty good customers.

Ralph   Well, we all sincerely *try* to be good customers. You can't do more than that, can you?

Mother   Just so long as you try to be good, dear, God will understand.

Heaven

Geoffrey	Another beautiful day. Heaven really looks at its best on a day like this.
Jean	Heaven always looks at its best.
Geoffrey	Yes, doesn't it. Every time I have to come up here to the Acts of God Directorate I'm rather . . . I don't know . . . *moved*. Those golden streets. That amethyst archway in front of the Recording Angel's office. I'm . . . oddly attached to this place, you know, Jean.
Jean	Aren't we all?
Geoffrey	You're very lucky here in Small Catastrophes. Having this view over the Major Disasters building. All these sapphires and chalcedonies and sardonyxes flashing in the sun. Every time I come up here for a meeting and see this view I'm oddly . . . I don't know . . .
Jean	Moved.
Geoffrey	Yes. Aren't you?
Jean	Of course.
Geoffrey	We're all very lucky, really. I can't help feeling sometimes that we're all rather . . . well . . .
Jean	Privileged to be here. Yes. All right, Geoffrey, what have I done wrong this time?
Geoffrey	(*laughs*) 'Done wrong'! Good. Yes. Very witty.
Jean	Well, then, what have I done less right that I should have?
Geoffrey	Jean, this chap you're going to kill in Norfolk.
Jean	You don't want me to kill him?
Geoffrey	Of course I want you to kill him. But you've got him down to be killed by an avalanche. Dear Jean, if you so wish, *of course*. But do you realise the cost of producing an avalanche in Norfolk? In terms of ecological damage and disruption of life? We'd have to throw up a complete range of mountains first!
Jean	Geoffrey, we must have this out once and for all. Whatever way I put forward to kill people it doesn't meet with your approval! I say, we'll drop a slate on his head. You immediately come running up here and say, do I

appreciate just how much wind we have to let loose to dislodge a slate? Geoffrey, I don't *care* how much wind we have to let loose, or how many mountains we have to push up! You see? It doesn't interest me.

Geoffrey Jean – dear Jean – my job, my humble task in this organisation, is to protect the innocent . . .

Jean And my job's to kill them! There's a definite policy clash here. Every method I come up with – tidal waves, giant hailstones, earth tremors – you try to block it!

Geoffrey Jean, Jean, Jean! I'm not blocking anything! All I'm saying is, does it have to be this particular man in Norfolk? Couldn't you bring the avalanche down on someone who lives at the foot of a mountain already?

Jean But that would be *banal!* The whole *point* of the operation is to enrich the texture of life! To engender a certain sense of wonder at the possibilities of the world! To keep alive a sense of awe! You must expect to make a few sacrifices for that.

Geoffrey Well, Jean, I think there's a lot to be said for the good, old-fashioned, well-tried . . .

Jean Flash of lightning.

Geoffrey Particularly in Norfolk.

Jean Oh, Geoffrey! I sometimes wonder if you really love me.

Geoffrey Of course I love you.

Jean As much as I love you?

Geoffrey As much as we all of us here love each other.

An Occasion of This Nature

Speaker   There always, I'm afraid, comes the dread moment at an occasion of this nature when someone gets up on his or her hind legs and makes a speech. That moment has now come! I know that the last thing anyone here wants to do is to listen to a speech, just when everyone was enjoying themselves, and the last thing *I* want to do is to make a speech, believe me, but I do think that we cannot let an occasion of this nature go by without stopping for just a moment to say a few words about how worthwhile and enjoyable an occasion of this nature is. We all take things for granted only too easily – I know I do – and I think if no one took the trouble to just stand up for a moment and put it into words, we might just possibly all sit here and not realise quite what a worthwhile and enjoyable time we were in fact having.

It cannot, I think, be said too often that an occasion of this nature doesn't just happen of its own accord. Let's all have a good time and enjoy ourselves, by all means. But let's try to bear in mind as we do so all the hard work and long hours and personal sacrifice that have gone into it. And I must just say here, before I forget, that Mr Pettigrew tells me there are still a great many tickets unsold for the Grand Lucky Draw. So can we all put our backs into it and make one last effort? There are some splendid prizes to be won, and anyway the prizes are not what counts. Oh yes, and would people *please* not put unwanted sandwiches or other matter into the heating vents? I know how easy it is for little fingers to do – perhaps even for fingers that *aren't* quite so little! – but getting small pieces of decaying fishpaste out again with knitting needles and surgical forceps, as we had to do last year, does waste a lot of the limited time available for committee meetings.

I should just like to say a word of thanks to the many people involved in making today a success, I'm sure that having their name mentioned was the last thing they had in mind in the first place, and they'll probably never forgive me, but I hope they'll forgive me if there are any names I forgot to mention.

First and foremost, of course, our heartiest thanks are due once again to Mrs Paramount. I'm sure I don't have to tell you that without Mrs Paramount an occasion of this nature simply could not take place. This is, in a very special sense, her baby – and has been so ever since the late Lord Combermere on his death bed first planted the seed.

Our thanks are also due, in no less measure, to Mr Huddle for his unfailing cheerfulness, and his apparent readiness in emergencies to dash almost anywhere in the middle of the night, clad in old army boots and Manchester United scarf. And I should like to say a special word of thanks to Mr Hapforth, who comes along here tonight against doctor's orders, and in spite of being in considerable pain. I think perhaps we might remember that when we see him struggling to entertain us all once again.

Last but not least I should like to thank all of you for coming along here today, and working so hard to enjoy the entertainment that all these good people have worked so hard to provide. It's particularly gratifying to see so many young faces. We often think of young people today as simply out for a good time. Well, that certainly can't be said of these young people. It's no less gratifying to see all the people here who aren't quite so young. I know how easy it is to think, 'Oh, let someone else go out this time and get themselves entertained.' I must say, it's remarkable how an occasion of this nature seems to bring out the best in people. Everyone rallies round and cheerfully tries to make the best of it. It's like the war all over again! I'd just like to say this: it's people like you who make an occasion of this nature the sort of occasion that it is. I'm sure you'll be pleased to hear that as a result of everyone's efforts today and over the past year we have raised the very gratifying total of £23.17.

Well, you don't want to sit here listening to me talk, and I certainly don't want to stand here talking, so I'm going to sit down and let Mr Dauntwater stand up and speak. Mr Dauntwater, I should explain, has kindly agreed at very short notice to make the speech thanking me for my speech. So, in the sudden but unavoidable absence of Mrs Hummer with gastric trouble, and to save time later on, I should just like if I might to thank Mr Dauntwater for his speech in advance. And thank you all for listening to me. And remember! Not in the heating vents!

The Messenger's Assistant

Enter **Meander,** *an ill-fated King.*

Meander   Oh, who would choose my hapless destiny?
To be a king, with naught to do but wait
For messengers from other parts of Greece
With mournful news of yet some fresh disaster;
Of madness in Thebes, of rape in Thessaly;
Of slow revenge and murder everywhere;
Of oracles predicting worse to come.
The signs portend another messenger
Today. What tragic tale will he unfold?
What solemn threnody of unseen woe?
But look! He is approaching even now!
And from from his face I fear the news will prove
More pain to bear than all the rest. Yet stay!
Someone comes with him. A woman. What is this?

Enter a **Messenger** *and his* **Wife.**

Messenger   O most unhappy king!
Wife   It's terrible!
Messenger   O ruler cursed by fate!
Wife   It's tragic, really.
I told them it would happen! I saw it coming!
Now put that sword away, I said, before
Some accident occurs. But would they listen?
Messenger   I am, O King, a messenger from Thrace . . .
Wife   And I'm his wife. I help him with his work.
I go on all his business trips – I have to!
He's hopeless if you leave him to himself!
He always gets the story wrong! Leaves out
The best bits – gets the point all back to front!
A messenger? I send him out to buy
A leg of lamb, and back he comes with goat!
Messenger   What is man's life? What is man's destiny?

Wife	Get on with it! He doesn't want to stand
	And wait all day while you philosophise!
Messenger	Know, then, ill-omen'd king, there stands in Thrace
	A grove of sacred alders by a brook,
	Where innocent maids delight to weave their
	garlands . . .
Wife	We had a picnic there the other week!
	We always like to get out when it's fine.
	We took some sandwiches – I made a cake.
	Just us. It was nice. Of course, we never *dreamed*!
Messenger	All unsuspecting to this guileless grove
	Came Ichtheumon, the son of Polyphonius . . .
Wife	Blood everywhere! You wouldn't believe the mess!
Meander	Ichtheumon! My cousin once removed? Is dead?
	Thus has the ancient prophecy been fulfilled!
Messenger	No, no!
Wife	No, no!
Messenger	Not Ichtheumon.
Wife	The other one!
Messenger	Diameter.
Wife	Diameter!
Meander	The son
	Of Radius? Can it be?
Messenger	It fell out thus:
	Unto the rustling alders in the grove
	Came Ichtheumon, and Agone, his sister . . .
Wife	Wearing a chlamys that her mother made
	From a tablecloth her aunt brought back from Persia.
Messenger	Now in this grove there sat a gnarled old man,
	And slowly, wondering much, they recognised
	In him Phlogiston, who was driven forth
	From Argos by a jealous royal house . . .
Wife	I'd like to hang them all, I really would.
Messenger	. . . For slaying Chloros, son of Aspidistra,
	In vengeance for the death of Rhododendron.
Wife	I hate to interrupt. I know how cross
	You get. But time and time again I've told you –
	Chloros wasn't Aspidistra's son,
	But Oxygenia's child by her first husband!
	She later married Neon. In white. Some people!

Meander	This is indeed a painful tale to bear.
Messenger	In any case, Phlogiston now was here,
	Fleeing the wrath of Archipelagos . . .
Wife	No, dear! Not Archipelagos at all!
	It was Parenthesis, for heaven's sake!
	You're muddling it with the job you had last week
	Of telling Oxymoron that his children
	Had been expelled from school for matricide!
Messenger	Fleeing the wrath of Archipelagos!
Wife	This is embarrassing! Quite how you got
	A job as messenger I can't imagine.
Messenger	The wrath belonged to Archipelagos!
	Another messenger told me this morning!
Wife	But he was probably just as bad as you!
	I don't suppose he had his wife with him
	To put him right on just this kind of detail!
Messenger	Excuse me.

He takes his **Wife** *off.*

Meander	Why do they always do it out of sight?

A scream, off.

We'll have a memorandum now on this!

Enter the **Messenger**, *alone.*

Messenger	At last! A bloody deed I can recount
	Without the slightest fear of interruption!